CULTURE SMART!

TANZANIA

Quintin Winks

·K·U·P·E·R·A·R·D·

This book is available for special discounts for bulk purchases for sales promotions or premiums. Special editions, including personalized covers, excerpts of existing books, and corporate imprints, can be created in large quantities for special needs.

For more information contact Kuperard publishers at the address below.

ISBN 978 1 85733 483 8
This book is also available as an e-book: eISBN 978 1 85733 605 4

British Library Cataloguing in Publication Data
A CIP catalogue entry for this book is available from the
British Library

First published in Great Britain
by Kuperard, an imprint of Bravo Ltd
59 Hutton Grove, London N12 8DS
Tel: +44 (0) 20 8446 2440   Fax: +44 (0) 20 8446 2441
www.culturesmart.co.uk
Inquiries: sales@kuperard.co.uk

Series Editor Geoffrey Chesler
Design Bobby Birchall

Printed in Malaysia

About the Author

QUINTIN WINKS is a Canadian journalist, freelance writer, and photographer. After graduating in journalism from the Langara College, Vancouver, he spent several years reporting for Canadian newspapers. His passion for writing and interest in culture led him to East Africa, where he based himself in Dar es Salaam, Tanzania. From his inner-city apartment, Quintin wrote monthly columns for the *Dar Guide* and contributed to Zanzibar's *Karibu* magazine, *This Day* newspaper, and *PAA*, Precision Airways' in-flight magazine, and used the rest of his time to explore East Africa.

Quintin has contributed to a variety of news and travel publications across North America. He has also published photography from Iceland to Botswana, Bolivia to the Canadian Arctic, and many cultures and landscapes in between. Now based on Vancouver Island and writing for a daily newspaper, his latest book project explores the decline of community news in North America.

**The Culture Smart! series is continuing to expand.
For further information and latest titles visit
www.culturesmart.co.uk**

The publishers would like to thank **CultureSmart!**Consulting for its help in researching and developing the concept for this series.

CultureSmart!Consulting creates tailor-made seminars and consultancy programs to meet a wide range of corporate, public-sector, and individual needs. Whether delivering courses on multicultural team building in the USA, preparing Chinese engineers for a posting in Europe, training call-center staff in India, or raising the awareness of police forces to the needs of diverse ethnic communities, it provides essential, practical, and powerful skills worldwide to an increasingly international workforce.

For details, visit www.culturesmartconsulting.com

CultureSmart!Consulting and **CultureSmart!** guides have both contributed to and featured regularly in the weekly travel program "Fast Track" on BBC World TV.

contents

contents

Map of Tanzania

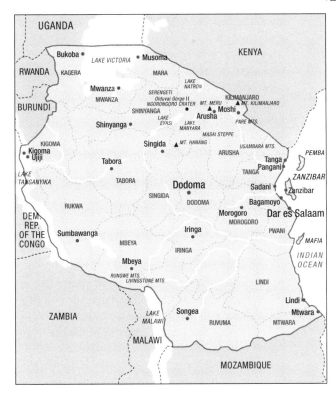

introduction

It is said that once Africa is in your blood, you will always return there. No expression could be more aptly applied to Tanzania. The country's harsh realities, its poverty, and its struggles, belie the rich, deep layers of culture that make it one of the most spectacular, impressive, and fascinating countries on the continent. Where else can you wake to a cup of outstanding Ethiopian coffee; lounge under a shady palm on a postcard-perfect beach; watch a dhow ply sapphire waters; and return to enjoy a breathtaking curry amid the muezzins calling the faithful to evening prayer?

There are many reasons to visit Tanzania, not least of which is to meet the Tanzanians. They are a mixture of the direct descendants of the first humans, of later tribes that migrated across Africa, and of people who arrived, eventually, from all over the world. Made up of some 120 tribes, most with their own language, the country is a melting pot of cultures and ethnicities.

If Tanzania is an exotic tapestry of flavors, colors, and smells, then the Tanzanians are the canvas that holds them all together. Collectively they have built a country where manners are valued, where handshakes are full of affection, and laughter is irrepressible. Warm, expressive, boisterous, engaging, peaceful, and, above all, friendly—there is no other people quite like them.

Gripe though you might, curse at the obstinacy, and swear at the inefficiency, once you've left you'll want nothing more than to return; because rare is a population whose national psyche is infused with such a spirit of helpfulness; where even a complete stranger will step forward to help someone in need. This is the quality of *undugu*, which permeates Tanzanian society and covers most of the country with a warm, effective social security blanket.

Perhaps that very same blanket also affords some emotional warmth. It would help to explain why physical contact between friends and acquaintances is a sign of respect and affection. It might also help to explain why Tanzania remains such a beacon of peace in East Africa, why it opens its doors to refugees, and why it has eluded the iron fist of a despotic ruler.

Tanzania is not content to remain among the world's poorest countries. It is striving, like a tide fighting upriver, to thwart corruption, streamline inefficiencies, eradicate illiteracy, and eliminate AIDS. As a result, it is a society in transition.

This book explores the country's past to explain some of the complexities and contradictions of modern Tanzanian society. It looks at how people relate to each other at home, at work, and at play, and offers advice on what to expect and how to behave in different contexts. Tanzanians are bighearted and optimistic. Make the effort to understand them, and they will welcome you unreservedly.

Key Facts

Official Name	United Republic of Tanzania	Combination of Tanganyika, mainland Tanzania's earlier name, and Zanzibar, after the two joined in 1964
Capital City	National capital Dodoma; financial capital Dar es Salaam	Dodoma became the capital in 1964. Dar es Salaam is still home to the central government bureaucracy.
Main Cities	Dar es Salaam, the biggest city and financial capital. Official pop. 2,497,940 (2002 census), but unofficial estimates closer to 4 million	Other main cities include Dodoma and Arusha.
Area	364,900 sq.miles (945,087 sq. km)	Inland water, incl. Lake Victoria, 22,799 sq.miles (59,050 sq. km). Coastline 885 miles (1,424 km) long
Borders	Tanzania is bordered by Kenya, Uganda, Rwanda, Burundi, Democratic Republic of the Congo, Zambia, Malawi and Mozambique.	
Climate	Varies with altitude, terrain, and season. Coast has av. daily temp. of 80–84°F (27–29°C); Arusha ranges from 56 to 86°F (13–30°C); average 77°F (25°C)	Jul.–Aug., winter; Jan.–Feb., dry/hot; Mar.–May, long rains; Jun.–Sept., dry; Oct.–Dec., short rains
Population	40,213,160 (2008 est.); growth rate 2.072%	43.5% under 14; av. life expectancy 51 years

Ethnic Makeup	Mainland: 99% African, 1% Asian, European, and Arab. Zanzibar: Arab, African, and a mix of the two.	Of the African population, 95% are Bantu, consisting of more than 130 tribes.
Currency	Tanzania shilling Tsh 1,315=1 USD	
Religion	Christianity and Islam have the most followers.	Also traditional beliefs, Hinduism, and Sikhism
Language	Swahili is the official lang.; English the main lang. of commerce, administration, and higher education.	Arabic is widely spoken in Zanzibar and there are several dozen local languages.
Literacy	69.4% of pop. over age 15 can read and write Swahili, English, or Arabic.	
Government	An independent republic with a unicameral National Assembly. President is head of state and head of government	Zanzibar elects a president who is head of government for matters internal to Zanzibar.
Electricity	220–240 volts (50 Hz)	Three-pronged plugs
Internet Domain	.tz	
Telephone	Country code 255	To phone abroad, dial country code and number.
Time	GMT +3 all year round.	Proximity to the equator means Tanzania gets about 12.5 hours of daylight year round, 5:30 a.m. – 6:00 p.m.

chapter one

LAND & PEOPLE

Tanzania is a land of wonder. It is sandwiched between the scorching equator, the Great Rift Valley—considered to be the "cradle of mankind"—and the absurdly blue Indian Ocean. It is home to Africa's highest mountain, deepest and largest lakes, and the Ngorongoro Crater, the biggest intact volcanic caldera on the planet. The Serengeti alone, one of the world's most famous national parks, hosts more amazing wild animals than all existing zoos combined. Meanwhile, Tanzania's rivers hide prehistoric reptiles and its plains support truck-sized pachyderms.

GEOGRAPHY

Tanzania is at the heart of East Africa. It borders Kenya and Uganda to the north, Rwanda and Burundi to the northwest, the Democratic Republic of the Congo to the west, Zambia to the southwest, and Malawi and Mozambique to the south. The Zanzibar archipelago forms the country's eastern boundary in the Indian Ocean, lying a little more than 18 miles (30 km) off the mainland, surrounded by white sand and electric blue water.

At 364,900 sq. miles (945,087 sq. km), Tanzania is almost four times the size of the United

Kingdom and about one-tenth that of the United States. Its main geographical feature is the Maasai Steppe, a large, semiarid plateau that rises more than 3,300 ft (1,000 m) above sea level. There are also three main mountain ranges—Pare and Usambara in the northeast and Livingstone in the southwest. Mount Kilimanjaro, near the northern border with Kenya, is Africa's highest mountain at 19,337 ft (5,894 m).

Kilimanjaro, along with Mount Meru, is a product of the East African rift system. The Great Rift Valley was born following a collision between two enormous tectonic plates about 30 million years ago. As the plates diverged following the collision, the earth's crust dropped back down between them, forming deep lakes and volcanic calderas. The valley runs north–south for some 4,039 miles (6,500 km) and is regarded by many archaeologists as humanity's birthplace.

To the northwest are Tanzania's great lakes. Lake Victoria is Africa's most extensive and Lake Tanganyika has the greatest depth, a maximum of 4,823 ft (1,470 m). Flowing into Lake Tanganyika is

the Kalambo River, which tumbles over Kalambo Falls, the second-highest waterfall in Africa with a single drop of well over 650 ft (200 m).

While the huge lakes and waterfalls are undoubtedly spectacular, it is Tanzania's national parks and game reserves that attract widespread international interest. The Serengeti is one of the world's most globally renowned parks. Its sprawling plains can be found in the country's northeast, along with nearby Ngorongoro Crater. Mikumi National Park and the Selous Game Reserve—the largest in Africa—are located in the central south of Tanzania and numerous smaller, lesser-known parks also dot the landscape. Gombe National Park, lying to the west, was made famous by Dr. Jane Goodall and her studies of chimpanzee behavior.

CLIMATE
Tanzania's climate is as varied as its geography, challenging travelers to come prepared for anything: the peak of Mount Kilimanjaro is

covered year-round by ice and snow, while the coast is hot and humid. The sun-baked, dry plains of the Maasai Steppe are in stark contrast to the cooler and greener mountain ranges.

Its location near the equator means that seasonal temperature changes in Tanzania are not extreme; winter and summer are both warm. Those unaccustomed to the tropics might find Tanzania hot, especially during the summer months from late December until February, while visitors to the coast might find the heat particularly wilting under a thick blanket of humidity. The winter months from late June to October are Tanzania's coolest. The short rains, so named because they tend to fall for little more than an hour or two each day, occur between October and December. The long rains, which can last days, are experienced March to May.

The coast and offshore islands are always warm, with an average year-round temperature of 80–84°F (27–29°C), though the Kasikazi and Kusi trade winds typically moderate this heat. In the central, northern, and western regions, the temperature, regulated by the highland plateau, ranges between 68 and 80°F (20–27°C) through June and August and there is low humidity, though it can reach the 86°F (30°C) level, higher between the months of December and March. In Tanzania's mountainous northeast and southwest the temperature occasionally drops below 59°F (15°C) at night during June and July. In the area around the Rungwe Mountains it can dip as low as 42°F (6°C).

Rainfall in the country's central region is sparse, usually less than 20 in (500 mm) annually; on the coast that jumps to between 39 and 74 in (1,000 and 1,900 mm). The mountains in the northeast and southwest also receive substantial rainfall, over 78.75 in (2,000 mm) falling annually.

FLORA AND FAUNA

Tanzania is one of Africa's premier wildlife watching destinations, with few other countries on earth offering such a diverse collection of big animals in such varied topography and climate. Though, in Africa as a whole, poaching and hunting have greatly reduced the numbers of animals, the Tanzanian government's progressive stance on preservation and sustainability means that creatures from elephants to honey badgers and leopards to flamingos remain easily accessible through world-class national parks and reserves. There are hundreds, if not thousands, of animal species within Tanzania and a similar range of birds. The mountains, jungles, plains, rivers, and lakes all offer abundant viewing of everything from insects to members of the big five: lions,

rhinoceroses, elephants, leopards, and buffalo. On the coast, rich mangrove swamps shelter fish and other ocean dwellers, while marine parks provide some of the best snorkeling anywhere. Palm trees nourish the rare coconut crab and colossal baobab trees ensure honeybees can produce their exotic nectar.

Meanwhile, colobus monkeys continue their mischief and butterflies of all shapes and sizes help to pollinate the forests.

PEOPLE

Tanzanians are typically native Africans, live in the countryside, and work in agriculture. They can trace their lineage from one of the 130 or so Bantu tribes in Tanzania and have an average life expectancy of 51 years (50 for men, 52 for women). Of the total population, 44 percent are aged under fourteen and 53 percent from fifteen to sixty-four, so there is only a tiny number of elderly. Statistically, Tanzanians are either Muslim or Christian and speak Swahili, a Bantu language with strong Arabic—and more recently English— infusions. Typically they are literate, though they are unlikely to have completed postsecondary education. While most Tanzanians fit all or part of this description, it is still a broad generalization. Additional numbers provide a more detailed picture of the population.

There are 40.2 million Tanzanian residents and all but some 400,000 are of African descent, the rest Asian, European, and Arab. Recent population estimates of the Asian community (including Hindus, Sikhs, Shia and Sunni Muslims, and Parsis) are 50,000 on the mainland and 4,000 on Zanzibar. An estimated 70,000 Arabs and 10,000 Europeans (most of whom were born in Africa) also reside in Tanzania.

Most native Africans indigenous to Zanzibar belong to one of three groups named after their island of origin: the Hadimu, found mostly in the south of Zanzibar; the Tumbatu, from Umbatu Island; and the Wapemba from Pemba Island.

The Zanzibar archipelago is a Muslim enclave; people of this faith account for 99 percent of the population.

Language and Identity

The majority of Tanzanians—roughly 95 percent—are speakers of Bantu languages. Each ethnic group, like the Hehe (Iringa region), Sukuma (Mwanza and southern Lake Victoria), and the Nyamwezi (Tabora region), has its own language and for most it is the members' first. But the national language is Swahili, which almost everyone speaks. English is considered an official language and is the primary language of commerce, administration, and higher education.

Also spoken are Indian languages, Portuguese (both by Mozambican blacks and Goans), and Arabic, which is still widely used on Zanzibar. Those who historically migrated south from the Nile River, known as Nilotic people, include the nomadic Maasai and, to a lesser extent, the Luo, though both are found in greater numbers in neighboring Kenya. Languages of the Khoisan family are specific to two small groups, the Bushman and Khoikhoi peoples. Migrants from the Ethiopian Highlands, such as the Iraqw and the tiny Gorowa and Burungi tribes, speak Cushitic. Other Bantu-speaking groups were refugees from Mozambique.

A BRIEF HISTORY
3.6 Million Years Ago
The history of Tanzania dates from long before the establishment of political boundaries, before written or oral records, even before modern man.

Between 1962 and 1964, archaeologists discovered some of the world's oldest evidence

of humans: bones dating from nearly two million years ago unearthed in and around Olduvai Gorge in northeast Tanzania. This area is often described as the "cradle of mankind." The Laetoli footprints, the earliest known of the immediate ancestors of humans, were also discovered in Tanzania and are estimated to be about 3.6 million years old.

8000–1000 BCE

Human settlement in what would eventually become Tanzania has progressed gradually since earliest times. Archaeologists believe that about 10,000 years ago the land was sparsely populated by hunter-gatherer societies, most likely Khoisan-speaking people. Five thousand years later, Cushitic speakers began to drift in from the Ethiopian Highlands and North Africa.

These tribes introduced basic techniques of agriculture, food production, and cattle farming. As time went by, they absorbed the hunter-gatherer communities of the region. Then, from about 1000 BCE, a cycle of migrations began that would alter the scope of human settlement on the landscape.

Of interest, the Hadzabe people form one of the oldest hunter-gatherer tribes in the world. They still live off the land in central and northern Tanzania.

A Scene from the Beginning of Mankind

A Hadzabe elder, his head and back covered with a single, magnificent baboon skin, crouches in the morning heat. Around him, a handful of tribesmen squat at the base of a ponderous baobab tree. The men are naked except for a few tattered remnants of cloth. Nearby, a group of women and children sit and chatter noisily in the dirt. Using the palms of his hands, one tribesman spins a stick into a piece of wood with the ease that comes with a lifetime of repetition. A wisp of smoke curls into a coil. A few breaths of air, some wood shavings, and the ember becomes a crackling fire.

1000 BCE–1800 CE

Bantu speakers from West Africa's Niger Delta began drifting east, arriving in Tanzania's Lake Victoria region as early as 1000 BCE. For the next nine centuries, they would continue to migrate, spreading over much of present-day Tanzania. They brought with them advanced agricultural techniques, ironworking skills, and new ideas of social and political organization. This large group slowly absorbed the Cushitic and the remaining pockets of Khoisan speakers. Eventually, smaller groups of Nilotic people started to arrive from southern Sudan, first fighting and then mixing with the area's Bantu speakers. This migration continued until about 350 years ago, with the most significant influxes taking place in the fifteenth and sixteenth centuries. Most Nilotic people, like the Maasai, were pastoralists and many settled in the less fertile areas of north-central Tanzania where their herds could graze.

Through this migration and evolution, an informal system of *ntemi* chiefdoms emerged. *Ntemi* is the Bantu word for chief. It comes from the verb *kutema*, which literally means to cut down trees or to clear bush. The chiefs were so named because of their early roles in blessing the land at the beginning of each cultivation season, when it was cleared. The name could also refer to the cutting short of arguments by village elders following an important discussion. Each chief had a council of advisers in a system that was structured, flexible, and benevolent. By the nineteenth century there were an estimated 200 or more chiefs in western and central Tanzania, presiding over a population of about 200,000 people.

The Coast

While migrant groups were trickling into Tanzania and the East African interior, recorded history was unfolding on the coast. It was here, on the shores of the Indian Ocean, that the outside world first collided with that of East Africa. This coastal area became known to Arab traders as Azania and later as the Land of Zinj, or the "Land of Blacks."

Permanent settlements sprang up along the Tanzanian coast as early as 1000 BCE. Traders from the Roman Empire and later from Persia and Arabia came ashore and began assimilating with the indigenous Bantu speakers. From this mix came both the Swahili language and its culture.

Swahili is derived from the Arabic word *sahil*, both meaning "of the coast." The Arabian traders also introduced Islam, which by the eleventh century had attracted a huge following. The heyday for these traders was between the thirteenth and fifteenth centuries, when trade in ivory, gold, and other goods spanned the Indian Ocean and beyond, reaching as far away as China.

THE LAND OF ZINJ

Despite constant quarrels amongst the coastal trading outposts, the Land of Zinj was a remarkable place. Its richer merchants lived in style, in spacious houses with broad verandahs and sunken courtyards overhung by trees and scented with oleander and jasmine. Interiors were softened with Persian carpets and finished in rosewood, inlaid with ivory. Around tables set with silver, crystal glassware, and Chinese porcelain, the men might sit clothed in gold-embroidered silks, their curved daggers, hilts encrusted with gems, tucked into silken sashes at the waist. Their women, segregated and in purdah, would have dressed in simple Islamic robes and headscarves. But beneath these modest garments might be bracelets, bangles, and necklaces, of gold and silver and studded with precious or semiprecious stones, a hidden concession to femininity. Enhanced, no doubt, by all the perfumes of Arabia.

G. Mercer, *Bagamoyo, Town of Palms*

When the Portuguese arrived at the end of the fifteenth century, they found East Africa's most powerful trade center at Kilwa Kisiwani. The Portuguese promptly plundered the wealthy city-state, originally established by Arab

traders. This marked the beginning of Portugal's brutal reign over the region. It was not until 1698 that the Portuguese were driven out, after Kilwa sought help from the Omani Arabs. The Omani Al Bu Said dynasty replaced the region's Yarubi leaders in 1741, and proceeded to develop trade further. It was during this time that Zanzibar gained its legendary status as a focus for the slave and ivory trades, becoming in 1841 the capital city of the sultan of Oman.

The European Explorers

While slaves—some 600,000 were sold through Zanzibar during the height of trading between 1830 and 1873—and ivory poured into the coast, European explorers set off in the opposite direction. From the 1850s, pioneers such as John Speke, Richard Burton, Henry Morton Stanley, and Dr. David Livingstone pushed into the heart of Africa. But with the age of European exploration of the continent came colonial domination.

SULTAN SEYYID SAID AND ZANZIBAR

Zanzibar became the hub of the Omani commercial empire and the principal staging point for the vast numbers of slaves it controlled. Each slave trader who wanted to bring his slaves through Zanzibar paid taxes into the sultan's coffers, and the overseas empire of Oman grew and grew. The most powerful of the Omani sultans was Seyyid Said. He took the throne aged just fifteen after assassinating his own cousin with a knife, and set about consolidating his power and tightening the Omani grip on Zanzibar.

Busy defending his interests in Oman, Seyyid did not make it to Zanzibar himself until well into his reign. When he did, sailing into the harbor on one of his magnificent warships in 1828, he was enchanted. Used as he was to the dry desert terrain of Oman, the sight of Zanzibar's tropical greenery filled him with delight. He decided to move his capital from Muscat to Zanzibar, taking his wives, concubines, and most of the Omani nobility with him.

Gemma Pitcher, *Magic of Zanzibar*

In 1822 the British imposed the Moresby Treaty on Sultan Seyyid Said in order to limit the slave trade in his African and Omani dominions, but it continued unabated until finally outlawed in 1873. The legal status of slavery was not abolished in Zanzibar until 1897. The USA, Britain, and France meanwhile established diplomatic relations with Zanzibar, which was the first territory in tropical Africa to enjoy such a connection. In 1861, following a dispute over the succession after the death of Seyyid, Zanzibar and Oman separated.

Zanzibari control of the East African coast was increasingly challenged by German colonial activity. In 1890 Britain obtained a protectorate over Zanzibar and recognized Germany's claims to the mainland. The colony of German East Africa was formally established in 1897. Following Germany's defeat in the First World War, the League of Nations gave most of German East Africa to Britain to govern as the mandated territory of Tanganyika, and it remained under Britain's purview for almost a half century.

Independence

British colonial rule in Tanganyika was relatively uneventful, though during the period a steady groundswell of nationalism began to emerge among Tanganyikans. Some of this derived from past injustices and resentment of partiality toward white settlers and Asians in the agricultural and business sectors. But it was the Second World War that really provided the impetus for independence. Some 100,000 native Tanganyikans fought for the Allies overseas and their exposure to other countries and

cultures increased their awareness of their status as second-class citizens at home. They had fought hard for democracy and against racism in Europe, yet came home to a country mired in racist and undemocratic policies.

The nationalist movement reached a crescendo in the early 1950s, following bitterness at the government's forcible relocation of the Meru tribe from western Kilimanjaro to make way for European farmers. Despite many appeals to authorities as elevated as the United Nations General Assembly, the Meru cause was rejected,  forcing them to turn to local political groups for support. These groups in turn looked to the Tanganyika Africa Association, or TAA, for leadership.

Into this environment stepped Julius Nyerere. After returning home from his Master's degree studies in Edinburgh in 1952, he became involved with the TAA. By 1953 it had evolved into a more political and nationalist organization with a strong following in the country. Later that year, Nyerere was selected as the organization's president: he was thirty-two.

Under his leadership, a new constitution was drawn up and introduced in 1954 (celebrated annually in Tanzania as Saba Saba Day), and the TAA became the Tanganyika African National Union, or TANU. Within a year Nyerere had quit teaching to become its full-time leader.

By the mid-1950s, Britain was considering increasing the level of self-government in

Tanganyika and approached TANU to participate in an election. TANU agreed, winning all but one seat in the country's first democratic elections in 1960. Then, in December 1961, Tanganyika attained self-government; Nyerere became prime minister, and president the following year. Not a drop of blood had been spilled.

Zanzibar was also granted full independence, in 1963. Its Arab government was toppled a month later and, in April 1964, Tanganyika and Zanzibar merged to become the United Republic of Tanzania. Nyerere continued as president, a position he held until 1985.

Post Independence

The first president is still remembered fondly today. Nyerere was always known as "Mwalimu," the Swahili word for teacher. He embraced socialism and looked to China for inspiration in forming postcolonial Tanzania—the results were economically disastrous.

Nyerere called for an overhaul of the economic system by means of African socialism and self-reliance in locally administered villages. The villagization program, implemented in 1973–6, sought to transform the pattern of rural settlement. The idea was that new, large villages would become the basis for a socialist system of production. The plan involved relocating people to purpose-built communal villages in the countryside, where every individual would be in the service of the community. These settlements were extremely unpopular and Nyerere eventually had to force people to move. This was just one of many reasons for the failure of "Ujamaa," Nyerere's form of agrarian socialism (see The Economy, below). To his credit, in the wake of this failure, Nyerere announced that he would retire after the presidential elections in 1985, leaving the country to enter its free-market era under the leadership of Ali Hassan Mwinyi.

In addition to economic reforms, Mwinyi was also instrumental in abolishing Nyerere's one-party rule. The law banning other political parties had been the result of a merger between Nyerere's TANU and Zanzibar's Afro-Shirazi Party (ASP) in 1977. Together, the two parties formed the Chama Cha Mapinduzi (or  CCM), which is still the governing party today. Having attained power with Nyerere at the helm, the CCM rewrote Tanzania's constitution. The law forbidding opposition parties was eventually overturned by Mwinyi in 1992. Today, the amended constitution allows for multiparty elections.

Zanzibar's semiautonomous status, combined with popular opposition, has led to two contentious elections there, in 2000 and 2005. President Salmin Amour was first elected in single-party elections in 1990, then reelected in 1995 in Zanzibar's first multiparty elections. His successor, Amani Abeid Karume, was elected in 2000 (amid violence and voting irregularities). Karume was reelected in 2005, once again amid accusations of voting irregularities.

On the mainland, the 1995 election saw Benjamin William Mkapa of the CCM rise to power as president. He was reelected in 2000 and served until 2005, when Mkapa was replaced

by the current president, Jakaya Kikwete. Today, Kikwete seems committed to fighting corruption and making every effort to usher in a new age of prosperity for Tanzanians. The vast majority of state-owned utilities and corporations have been privatized and Kikwete's government is working to encourage foreign and domestic investment.

GOVERNMENT

Tanzania is governed under the amended constitution of 1992. The president, who is head of state and head of government, is elected by popular vote for a five-year term and is eligible for a second.

The legislature's single chamber consists of the 274-seat National Assembly, known as the Bunge; 232 members are popularly elected, 37 are women appointed by the president, and 5 are members of Zanzibar's legislature (Zanzibar has its own president and House of Representatives, for dealing with matters internal to the island). All legislators serve five-year terms. Administratively, Tanzania is divided into twenty-six regions.

CITIES

Dar es Salaam is the capital of Tanzania in everything but name. This city of 2.5 million residents (unofficial population estimates are close to 4 million) is the economic, cultural, business, and population hub of the country.

Until the mid-eighteenth century Dar es Salaam was a small and uninspiring town, and then the sultan of Zanzibar decided to develop it into a port and trading center, endowing it with its present name, which means "haven of peace."

The advent of big, deep-sea steamships led the Germans, in 1891, to move their colonial capital from Bagamoyo, some 38 miles (60 km) to the north, to Dar es Salaam. Its natural deepwater harbor facilitated docking of the large vessels.

Affectionately known as Dar, the city has remained the undisputed de facto capital of Tanzania, even though the official seat of government was transferred to Dodoma in 1973. Dodoma is centrally situated about 250 miles (400 km) west of Dar, along a once important caravan route that connected Central Africa with the coast. Today it is a relatively sleepy, laid-back city of 150,000 residents. Convoys of 4WDs herald periodic legislative meetings.

In the north lies Arusha, Tanzania's safari capital and one of the country's fastest-growing cities. It's the jumping-off point for the Serengeti,

Ngorongoro, and Kilimanjaro National Parks and enjoys a temperate climate year-round, thanks to its 4,200 ft (1,300 m) elevation.

There are smaller cities in the more remote areas of Tanzania: Morogoro, Tabora, Iringa (center), and the deep northwestern (Mwanza) and western (Mbeya) fringes of the country. Some of these date from the days of the caravan routes, when they were important resupply stops.

THE ECONOMY

Like just about any society that has endured a major shift in political and economic ideology, Tanzania has some entrenched inefficiencies. Its near bankruptcy, preceding the move to a free-market economy in 1986, led to a tripling of illiteracy rates and falling standards of education.

The majority of the poor still lack the necessary skills to exploit any new economic opportunities stemming from the free market and therefore struggle to raise their living standards. Disease, the lack of clean drinking water, and ongoing incidents of corruption at all levels also conspire to prevent Tanzania from surging ahead.

TheTanzanian economy is overwhelmingly agricultural. Plantations grow cash crops such as coffee, tea, cashews, tobacco, and sugarcane, but much of the population is engaged in subsistence farming. Still, the future looks good. Tanzania is moving in the right direction—as evidenced by renewed support from donor countries—with significant progress in structural and macroeconomic reforms.

Currency

Tanzania's currency is the shilling, written as either Tsh, TZS, or as a forward slash and hyphen following the number, for example 500/-.

Inflation in Tanzania is volatile, in the last five years dipping to 3.5 percent and spiking at around 7 percent. Due to this relative instability, there are two currencies circulated within Tanzania. In addition to the shilling, many prices are quoted in the US dollar because it is perceived as more stable. Interestingly, prices quoted in dollars are sometimes lower than their shilling equivalent.

Economic Standing

In 2005, Tanzania was ranked, based on the annual value of all goods and services produced per individual, in the bottom twenty countries in the world. Thirty-six percent of the population lives below the poverty line. Pinpointing the exact reasons for this situation is a lengthy exercise, though many blame the early socialist economic policies of Julius Nyerere, dating from Tanzania's independence in 1961.

Nyerere, we have seen, introduced a policy of collectivization in the country's agricultural system. He based his concept of Ujamaa on an age-old social model in Tanzania whereby the extended family supports its members, and in which the individual becomes a person through the people or community. He believed that Africans were socialists by nature and all that was needed for the country's success was to return to that traditional model of life.

By 1976 it had become obvious that Ujamaa was not working. It had failed to boost agricultural output and Tanzania had gone from the largest exporter of agricultural products in Africa to the continent's largest importer. These days, Tanzania needs to import fewer agricultural products, though consumer goods, machinery and transportation equipment, industrial raw materials, and crude oil are all necessary imports to keep the country functioning.

Even though Tanzania continues to be near the bottom of lists ranking the world's economies, there is cause for hope. Many of the country's public corporations are being privatized. The economy is slowly beginning to climb out of the depths of bankruptcy, where it once languished, tourism is booming, and Tanzania is routinely applauded by the international donor community for its progress.

On the Street

Though the average Tanzanian's income is low, visitors to the bigger cities might feel some

disconnect between that figure and reality. It seems most people are well dressed, big houses and fancy cars are common, and even the poorest of the poor seem to have cell phones. Business is always brisk at the local markets and those without shops have roadside kiosks, drive taxis, or work in hotels. But this is a relatively thin veneer. Look past the glitz into the poorer neighborhoods and desperate poverty is clearly evident. In rural areas some of the poorest people live without electricity or clean running water, windows, or sometimes even walls.

Agriculture

Tanzania's economy depends heavily on agriculture, which accounts for more than 40 percent of GDP, provides 85 percent of exports, and employs 80 percent of the workforce. Cashew nuts are the most obvious cash crop because of their ready availability on just about any city street in the country, though coffee, tea, cotton, sisal, cloves, and pyrethrum (a natural insecticide made from chrysanthemums) combine with cashews to account for the vast majority of export earnings.

The volume of all major crops has increased in recent years, but poor pricing and unreliable cash flow to farmers continue to undermine the agricultural sector.

Industry

Tanzania's industrial sector, at about 10 percent of GDP, is proportionally one of the smallest in

Africa. It produces raw materials, import substitutes, and processed agricultural products, such as sugar, beer, cigarettes, and sisal twine. Foreign exchange shortages, coupled with corruption, continue to deprive factories of essential spare parts and industrial capacity, by some estimates, has been reduced to less than 30 percent of pre-independence levels in the early 1960s.

Tourism

Tourism in Tanzania is expanding explosively, due in large part to the country's spectacular scenery and wildlife and the government's progressive view of protecting these natural resources with numerous national parks and wildlife refuges. Relatively recent fears that the famous snows of Mount Kilimanjaro will vanish within the next few decades have sparked a mountaineering rush. In the past fifteen years tourism has risen to nearly double the GDP of the industrial sector, making it the fastest-growing industry in the country.

TANZANIA WITHIN AFRICA

Since independence, Tanzania has been one of the most stable democracies in East Africa. That, and its proximity to Rwanda, made it the haven for more than one million refugees fleeing the Rwandan conflict of 1994. While the vast majority of Rwandans have been repatriated, Tanzania continues to provide shelter to nearly a half million refugees from a variety of African countries. This is one of the largest refugee populations in the world.

The same features made Tanzania the logical choice as host for the Rwandan genocide trials, which have continued for more than a decade in Arusha, yielding multiple convictions against those accused of perpetrating the violence.

Tanzania is also a significant player as a member of the East African Community (EAC). This body was originally created in 1967, after historic cooperation between the five member countries (Kenya, Rwanda, Burundi, Uganda, and Tanzania) dating from the early twentieth century. Though it collapsed in 1976, the EAC was revived in 1999.

The future of Tanzania within the EAC is for the time being uncertain. Having the lion's share of the Community's land, Tanzanians fear plans to transform the body into the East African Federation, a proposal that would see a common currency, passport, judicial branch, and legislature. A recent vote showed that Tanzanians fear residents of other member countries might use the increased freedom of movement as a land grab opportunity. As a result, plans to fast-track the Federation have been slowed, if not shelved.

VALUES & ATTITUDES

UNDUGU

No other philosophy conveys the Tanzanian spirit more than that of *undugu*. Meaning brotherhood, the word broadly includes the notions of extended family, generosity, consideration, and compassion toward others in the family and community. It refers, obliquely, to the social safety net: the haves share with the have-nots and one person who is working might support a dozen friends and relatives who are not. For most Tanzanians it is inevitable that a long-lost relative will eventually materialize and ask for a job, money for a son's medical treatment, or a place to stay. As might be expected, this sometimes causes a bit of grumbling.

Undugu, politics, and Ujamaa

We have seen that Julius Nyerere thought that the future of Tanzania lay in socialism. When he came to power in 1964, he modeled his particular brand of it on *undugu*. He believed that enforcing *undugu* would pave the country's way to prosperity, saying that the African extended family was the basis of a community where cooperation and collective advancement were the responsibility of every individual. He expanded these principles (in order to counter greed and materialism) and named the resulting concept Ujamaa. This he set out in the Arusha Declaration of 1967.

> **FROM THE ARUSHA DECLARATION**
> "The objective of socialism in the United Republic of Tanzania is to build a society in which all members have equal rights and equal opportunities; in which all can live in peace with their neighbors without suffering or imposing injustice, being exploited, or exploiting; and in which all have a gradually increasing basic level of material welfare before any individual lives in luxury."

In order to achieve Ujamaa, Nyerere forced his people into rural, collective farming villages. But the scheme backfired. Those who had been settled in these villages missed their relatives, weddings, religious rituals, and, not least, beer parties, all of which provided a break from the tedious farm work. And it was not long before people began growing their own food to raise income.

So, the collectivization program can be largely blamed for the failure of Ujamaa, along with the 1970s oil crisis, the steep fall in commodity prices, and the beginning in 1978 of a costly war with Uganda. The collapse of Ujamaa led to Nyerere's resignation and paved the way for Tanzania's gradual departure from socialism.

Yet this political ideology, and more specifically *undugu*, may nevertheless have contributed to Tanzania's unique stability in East Africa. In the days since its independence from colonial rule, the country has enjoyed (apart from its—provoked by Idi Amin—invasion of Uganda) almost uninterrupted peace, free of civil wars, violent coups, and aggressive foreign policy: all this despite a broad mixture of cultures, religions, and political beliefs coexisting under a single president.

STATUS

Like most societies, status in Tanzania today is attached to wealth and power—these, most often, are in the male domain. In this patriarchal society, women have less status than their husbands.

Status based on money and education is a relatively new and quite complex phenomenon, especially in the cities. Tanzanians are quite class conscious and members of the upper class will usually speak very firmly and directly to people in

an inferior position. A person of lower social standing will not usually look a person of higher status in the eye. Yet foreigners, regardless of their status, are not expected to avert their eyes. Tanzanians—especially women from rural areas—will sometimes do so when speaking with a visitor. In deference, some people might address you directly in the third person (for example "Would Mr. Brown like something to drink?").

Until recently, government was the main employer across the country. Politicians, businessmen and women, and workers are all consigned to their own classes. The workers fit into three categories: highly skilled government and private institution employees; middle-class civil servants; and low-paid workers.

For most Tanzanians, belonging to the lower class is simply a fact of life. Rarely are people ashamed of it, nor are they embarrassed to admit that someone is poorer or richer than them. Yet, in social situations, each knows their place and behaves accordingly. For instance, upper- or middle-class people do not usually frequent the same restaurants as their inferiors, even though they may eat the same food. Instead, they will send out a colleague with a container to bring them lunch.

There are few clues for outsiders pointing to someone's social class because many Tanzanian city dwellers live in sprawling, unplanned suburbs. Most people live or squat in these areas without identifying themselves by class. It is only the politicos, and often expatriate Westerners, who tend to live in a city's planned districts.

What's more, perhaps because of *undugu*, ostentatious wealth is rarely seen.

Regardless of the size or source of someone's income, whether the latter is a large inheritance or modest entrepreneurial skills, respect, manners, and sincerity will pave the way for productive interactions.

In rural Tanzania, historically local tribes were governed by chiefs and their councils of elders, presiding over societies of up to 2,000 people. With the arrival of colonialism these chiefdoms were largely abolished. Chiefs still exist among some of the most rural and traditional groups, however, where they enjoy great status.

"The Big Man"

Probably because of Tanzania's patriarchal past, there is still dutiful reverence toward the highest politicians in the land, inevitably men. Since its early history, Tanzania's families, tribes, and localized societies have been under male guidance and leadership. As a result, there is an ingrained respect for the government leaders and even businessmen. Few people will speak negatively, at least in public, of the president or his policies.

Asians and Caste Systems

Within Tanzania's bigger cities, there are sizable Asian populations who have immigrated, for the most part, from India and Pakistan. Many brought their caste systems from home. While marriages still often stay within caste, attitudes are changing. Increasing numbers of young people of Asian descent are eschewing the system, looking outside their castes for greater choice in the selection of a spouse.

WOMEN

The difficulties for women in Tanzania's patriarchal society begin at a young age. The practice of female circumcision is waning, but in some rural areas remains a tribal custom applied to girls from childhood through to early adulthood. Also called "cutting," this is performed primarily to reduce sexual pleasure in the adult woman, and for other cultural reasons. It most often involves the partial or total removal of the external female genitalia, but can feature more extensive damaging surgery. The health consequences can be extremely serious. The Tanzanian government, along with foreign aid agencies, is doing its best to eradicate the practice, though "cutting" continues to this day.

The disparity in status between the genders today is rooted in generations of patriarchal society. Women living in Tanzania are heavily marginalized. Their inferior education and literacy rates are reflected by their low profile in national politics and business.

There has been a recent resurgence of the *hijab* (the head covering or modest dress for Muslim women), which in Tanzania usually takes the form of a scarf hiding all but the face. Nevertheless, Tanzanian Muslim women are thought to enjoy more social freedom than in stricter Muslim countries. Marriage legislation introduced in the 1970s overrides customary and Islamic law, giving women far more latitude in divorce, remarriage, and inheritance matters.

Recent efforts by the government have improved the status of Tanzanian women in general. It passed a bill in 2000 to increase the number of women's seats in parliament and introduced regulations to include women in decision making at the national level. It has also publicly renounced discrimination against women.

While women vote, produce goods for market, engage in trade, and keep some of their earnings, the campaign against discrimination is mostly a fight in the public sphere. In reality, life for most women is still far from easy. Division according to gender of day-to-day labor depends on the tribe and the household, but women often raise children, do the housekeeping, tend crops, and fetch water. Some case studies show women doing up to 85 percent of the work required to support the family. That said, in the bigger cities especially, women are beginning gradually to play more important roles in business and society.

TANZANIAN IDENTITY

There is a multitude of tribes in Tanzania, yet very few individuals identify themselves by tribe. Almost universally they define themselves as Tanzanians, united by their national language, Swahili. This is a legacy of the Nyerere years. Yet the majority of people are also proud of their tribal heritage and will reminisce fondly about village life. For most Tanzanians, these are the collective memories of the twelve major ethnic groups that make up half the population.

Thanks also to Nyerere's policies, no single ethnic group dominates politically in Tanzania—the direct result of which has been continuous peace. Compared with neighboring countries, that is quite an achievement. In December 2007, Kenya descended to the brink of civil war as the Kikuyu and Luo tribes fought over land; in 1994 Rwanda suffered genocide between the Hutu and the Tutsi tribes; and in the 1970s, military dictator Idi Amin scarred Uganda with ethnic persecution and political murders.

Tribal ethnicity has considerable bearing on how two people address each other. Whether they are family or not, those from the same village typically call each other brother, sister, mother, grandmother, and so on.

Learning the various tribal reputations (for instance the Chagga are perceived as business savvy meat eaters who love beer, while the Sukuma, the country's largest ethnic group, are thought of as gentle and soft-spoken) can help a foreigner decipher some of the underlying dynamics of workplace relationships among Tanzanians.

Second in size to the Sukuma are the Makonde, who are based in the south, followed by the Chagga, who live in the shadow of Mount Kilimanjaro. While not the biggest group, the Maasai are the most visually spectacular. These seminomadic pastoralists wear traditional robes of vibrant reds and blues. They are usually very tall and lean, with plaited hair and bead jewelry, and consider both the land and the cattle to be sacred. The young warriors carry their traditional weapons and have a reputation for fierceness. These days, a great many young Maasai warriors are hired as security guards in the cities.

Arabs are considered to be different from indigenous Tanzanians, which might explain the cultural distance between the mainland and Zanzibar. Indians, who form a large part of Tanzania's business-owning class, are sometimes perceived as taking advantage of the native population and are resented for this. Despite this, there is generally a peaceful relationship with indigenous Africans.

NATIONAL PRIDE

Tanzanians are proud of their country. Though they may complain about it, you should refrain from joining in. Genuine praise for Tanzania and its residents will most often elicit warm smiles and sometimes a new friend. As with many peoples, there is a strong sense of pride associated with the land beneath their feet and the flag flying over their heads.

Also, avoid criticism of the government. Tanzanians are passionate about their politics and while that passion sometimes manifests itself as nothing more than boisterous debate, it can also become violent, as it did in the 2000 Zanzibar election.

Finally, Tanzanians do not appreciate being compared or confused with Kenyans. Doing so can hinder a potential friendship.

EMOTIONS IN PUBLIC

Tanzanians pride themselves on being calm and rational, two characteristics that can sometimes come across as cool or distant. These traits help explain why they are averse to displays of strong emotion in public. For instance, it is rare to see overt displays of anger. Most try to hide annoyance in the presence of their colleagues to avoid being seen as cowardly or intolerant. Therefore many people tend to smile and keep quiet when they might be hurt or upset. Even when indignation is at risk of overflowing, most Tanzanians voice their displeasure as a brusque and surprisingly effective "Tsk!"

Still, tempers do sometimes boil over and it is not unusual to see people having an argument with raised voices on the street, though this is not generally acceptable. Scores of spectators may throng to watch and some may mediate to help settle the dispute. This cools passions in a society that often cannot rely on police intervention.

Few men shed tears in public, unless they are really overcome with emotion, and even then it is typically a very brief lapse. Women are more likely to show their feelings, to some degree at least; for them, bouts of crying are seen as unusual but not worrying.

Expressions of sadness are encouraged in a context where they might be expected, however. Mourners attending a funeral will cry, sometimes noisily and for long periods of time, even if they did not know the deceased.

Space Invaders

Tanzanians have a different perception of personal space from Westerners. There is typically less distance between people than you might be used to and Tanzanians tend to stand even closer when having a dialogue. Keeping your distance from someone sends a signal that they are not welcome.

In a crowd, such as at the market or on a bus, there is virtually no allowance for personal space. Your neighbors may sometimes bump you—often unavoidable—but are not likely to apologize.

As with anger, public displays of affection are disapproved of. Kissing, holding hands, and hugging on the street are not acceptable. Most Tanzanians regard this sort of behavior by couples as boastful showing off.

Perhaps surprisingly, friendly affection between members of the same sex is considered perfectly fine. Tanzanian men, for example, will often hold hands long after the initial handshake is complete as a sign of fondness and respect.

Homosexuality, however, is not only taboo in Tanzania, it is also illegal. Though it exists, of course, any indication in public will not be appreciated, so exercise extreme caution.

HOSPITALITY

Tanzanians are warm, friendly people who sometimes welcome strangers with acts of enormous kindness. As a visitor to Tanzania, you can expect to receive offers of help from friends, distant acquaintances, and complete strangers alike—*undugu* in practice. This may be anything from assistance finding an apartment to simply providing directions.

But also be aware that, while some of these offers are sincere, others may be made with ulterior motives. When someone seems to be making a particularly special effort on your behalf, it is prudent to be up-front and establish what their motivation might be. The offer may well be made in the expectation of some form of remuneration.

Tanzanians are also conservative and unhurried. Coupled with their warmth and sincerity, this makes them one of the most egalitarian and tolerant societies in Africa. Add humor and kindness and this combination of traits endears Tanzanians to many visitors.

BEING A *MZUNGU*

Visitors to Tanzania will sometimes experience something like celebrity status. Often complete strangers will call out or approach in the street and begin a conversation. Thanks to a highly efficient word-of-mouth network, strangers will know your name or that of your friends. On other days it seems as though each taxi, solicitor, or money changer is pushing for a sale and every second person calls out "Hey, *mzungu*."

While this is initially a little wearying, by saying hello, by addressing you by name, by honking at you—the most tiresome one of all—Tanzanians are advertising themselves. They are trying to make their presence known, perhaps to create the basis of a friendship in the hope of it leading to work or other mutually beneficial arrangements.

Mzungu, literally translated, means a person who walks in circles. It is the name reserved for Westerners and it is advisable to abandon any irritation with the tag early in your stay: depending on the length of your visit, you might hear it thousands of times.

The "celebrity" treatment arises from several factors. Caucasians, in particular, stand out. Their white skin is the color of Hollywood movie stars and their cameras and designer clothes would be unimaginably expensive for many Tanzanians. As a result, Westerners are typically perceived as having bottomless bank accounts and exalted lifestyles. And, compared with a Tanzanian living in abject poverty, most visitors do. But it is worth remembering that your wealth is judged less by the money actually in your pocket than by the knowledge that, as a Westerner, you could fly home tomorrow and earn more in eight hours than many Tanzanians in a year.

"SWAHILI TIME"

"Swahili time" is based on a clock that is six hours behind. Ironically, this was done to simplify the process of telling the time. In "Swahili time" dawn coincides with twelve o'clock—06:00 to the rest of the world—and every hour afterward measures the time since dawn. Dusk is the same: sunset is at 12 o'clock—18:00.

"Swahili time" is unofficial, sort of. Governments and schools measure time in the universal fashion, along with the rest of the planet. But almost every Tanzanian is also familiar with "Swahili time" and some use it to organize their days. This is particularly important to remember when arranging for a taxi. If you tell the driver you need a ride to the airport at 6:00 (in the evening), there is a very good chance he will show up six hours earlier, at noon. And if you are expected for a meeting at half past one (meaning lunchtime), it is best to confirm the time to avoid any confusion.

WORK/LIFE BALANCE

Tanzanians place greater importance on free time than many Western cultures. That means work sometimes comes second to leisure or family time. Add to that a common lack of skills and training, a lack of ambition, and the result is a work ethic that is somewhat relaxed: many Tanzanians will work if they have to and won't if they don't. They are happy to work for the necessities and spend the most important time with their families or at leisure.

It is an exception for Tanzanians to work long hours. Stores that remain open twenty-four hours are extremely rare: almost all close at 5:00 p.m. As a result, after the evening rush hour has waned, many city centers are quiet (though far from deserted).

The motivation to earn a salary stems primarily from the Tanzanians' desire to fulfill their family obligations, which can be very heavy. However, when the qualifications and experience of those with higher education are put to use, they are more likely to be motivated by job satisfaction and commitment to the issues at hand. Prestige is based on position and place of employment.

Years spent as one of the poorest nations in the world means that Tanzanians can do incredible amounts of work when necessary, however. It usually takes just a glimpse of some people's daily grind for this realization to sink in. Women work particularly hard, sometimes caring for the family and supporting it financially at the same time.

Pole Pole

Pole pole (pronounced: "polay polay"), meaning slowly slowly, is a popular expression among Tanzanians. It can apply to many moods and situations and is often used humorously, especially when describing what Tanzanians perceive as their own inefficiency. Sometimes it is said disdainfully, directed, for instance, at another driver's aggression or at overt signs of impatience. On a different occasion it might be expressed joyfully, like over a cold drink after working hours. It may also be used with concern, for those who are clumsy, or to describe one's own feelings, or an approach to a problem.

Taken on its own, *pole pole* can be used to describe an aspect of the Tanzanian disposition: patient and calm with an emphasis on slowing down and enjoying life.

KITU KIDOGO

Likely the product of low wages, inadequate education, and a ponderous bureaucracy, the expectation of bribes is woven into Tanzanian culture. Newspapers delight in running stories of corruption in the upper levels of government—which acts as an "if-they-can-do-it-so-can-I" catalyst for the rest of the population. Tanzanians will regularly face bureaucratic roadblocks caused by inefficient procedures, or rules that were specifically created by state officials in search of a little side income. These they bear stoically with the knowledge that sometimes, in order to get something done, palms need a little grease.

The most common way to ask for that grease is *kitu kidogo*, which means in Swahili "a little thing."

It is frequently used by the traffic police when hesitating to give a fine, offering instead to ignore that you were speeding. In daily talk the Tanzanians also use words like *chai* (tea), or simply "I'm hungry," while pointing to the stomach.

While this bribery economy is prevalent at so many levels of Tanzanian society, most casual visitors feel the impact only in dealing with officials, particularly immigration authorities and police. Always be exceptionally polite. For petty offences, like driving without headlights switched on, police will often try to solicit a bribe, disguised as an on-the-spot fine.

Whether to participate is up to the individual, but to avoid paying the trick is to keep your hands out of your pockets. Take the time to establish the amount being requested, then offer to go to the police station to pay, at which point you should be released with a warning. It might seem obvious, but at no time should you wave money around.

FAMILY AND THE SOCIAL SAFETY NET

As we have already seen, Tanzanians who have are expected to share with those who do not. This attitude is largely due to the absence of a social security system, which places the burden of costs for education and health directly onto families. Only about one million people have access to any kind of formal social security, leaving a labor force of some sixteen million people forced to rely on family members in times of adversity.

Family Appeal

In Tanzania, my brother could be your third cousin and my mama is maybe your aunt. To the Tanzanians it means family. Your family is so huge that they are the people you go to in times of adversity. If you need a job, you ask the uncle who has connections, or his friend whom you also call uncle. If you need money, you go to mother, father, aunt, uncle, or older brother . . . the list is unending. It is always the extended family that saves your skin. Every time. And if you are higher on the pyramid, you become helper not helpee!

Sameer Kermalli, editor, *Desk Top Publishing*, Dar es Salaam

Meanwhile, there has been a slow but steady disintegration of the family-based social support systems on which the majority of Tanzanians have depended for help in emergencies. Economic hardship has made it difficult for individuals, families, and communities to provide assistance to each other in times of crisis. In addition, the high rate of urbanization has taken its toll on traditional social protection systems. Families have become more fragmented as they have been increasingly dispersed, eroding the capacity of extended families to function as social safety nets.

That said, the Tanzanian government is aware of the problem and continues to work toward a universal system of social security. To this end, urban centers have government hospitals where free emergency medical treatment is available, though conditions can be brutal. Charity and aid-funded hospitals will also provide most services free of charge.

ATTITUDES TO VIOLENCE AND CRIME

Tanzania has demonstrated a remarkably benign foreign policy (the provoked invasion of Uganda notwithstanding) and its domestic policies have a similar history, which goes some way to explain Tanzanians' attitudes toward violence and crime. The brutal dictatorships, civil wars, and ruthless militias found to varying degrees in most neighboring countries have never succeeded in Tanzania, though the deaths of several dozen Zanzibaris in election violence marred the record of the country's governing CCM party in 2000.

Still, Tanzanians are a reserved and rational people who resist overt displays of anger and violence. The one exception to this general rule is their treatment of petty crime. Though a daily reality in Tanzania's big cities, and to a lesser extent in rural areas, it is not taken lightly, and vigilante justice fills the gaps in policing. Thieves and criminals who are caught face severe beatings, and sometimes even death, at the hands of ordinary members of the public.

But what constitutes theft, exactly, is somewhat blurred by a culturally different perception of ownership. Being desperately poor, Tanzanians tend to view the removal of anything from the possession of an individual as blatant theft. Where the matter becomes something of a debate is in the area of fraud: once the money has left your hands, it is virtually impossible to get it back.

chapter three

BELIEFS, CUSTOMS, & TRADITIONS

RELIGIOUS DIVERSITY

Most Tanzanians are religious, and religion permeates the entire fabric of Tanzanian society. For many it is not just a set of beliefs but a way of life, the basis of culture, identity, and moral values. On the mainland, it is estimated that about 40 percent of the population are Christian, 40 percent are Muslim, and 20 percent follow traditional native beliefs. There are also some Hindus, Sikhs, and Ismailis. On Zanzibar, more than 99 percent of the population are Muslim.

Traditional African culture sometimes finds expression within the imported religions of Islam and Christianity. So, for example, it is not unusual for some Christians to have more than one wife, or for a Muslim to drink beer during important social ceremonies, such as weddings and funerals. Individuals are entitled to believe in anything, as long they do not break the state laws.

Tanzania is a model of religious coexistence: presidential candidates are chosen, in part, according to their religions and presidents are chosen in order to alternate faiths at the highest level. This is to ensure that Tanzania's two main religions—Islam and Christianity—are equally represented. The current president, Jakaya

Kikwete, a Muslim, succeeded President Mkapa, who is Catholic. Each president, in turn, appoints a fairly even balance of Muslim and Christian officials to government positions.

In addition to statutory legislation, Tanzanian courts apply the laws according to the religious affiliations of those before the courts. Christians are governed by customary and statutory laws in both criminal and civil cases. Muslims are subject to these laws in criminal cases only. In civil cases involving family matters such as marriage, divorce, child custody, and inheritance, Islamic law is used if both parties are Muslim and if they agree to be so adjudicated. If the parties are of different faiths, then statutory law applies.

ISLAM

Especially by the sea, and even more so on Zanzibar, Islam holds sway over Tanzanian life. Ruined thousand-year-old mosques sprinkled along the coast hint at Islam's long history here, though precisely when it surpassed traditional beliefs in popularity is unclear. Islam arrived on the shores of Tanzania with the first Arab traders. By the nineteenth century, the faith began migrating along the caravan routes, establishing roots in important trade depots such as Ujiji and Tabora.

The first, and most obvious, signs of Islam in Tanzania are the muezzins. Five times daily they call Muslims to prayer from the minaret of the local mosque. In the cities, where mosques are squeezed together, different Islamic sects advertise for new followers. This is done by building high minarets and installing powerful loudspeakers. The more potential adherents that can be reached over a greater range, the better. The alarmingly loud calls to prayer begin at 5:00 a.m.

Down on the street, Muslims are often easy to spot because of their *thawbs* (ankle-length robes) and the linen or muslin prayer caps—called *taqiyahs*—that they often wear with them. When worn by itself, the *teqiyah* can be any color but under the *keffiyah* scarf it is always white. Relaxing over a hookah pipe in the heat of the equatorial night is arguably the finest time to absorb the Muslim culture as long robes blend with long shadows on their way to or from the mosques.

Shoes must be left at the door of mosques and men wear a *taqiyah*. Within mosques, men and women pray separately.

In less strict Muslim areas, such as Dar es Salaam and other large centers, women are typically covered up with exception of the face and sometimes the head. In more traditional places they wear the *hijab*. Muslim women sometimes sport intricate henna tattoos on their hands and feet.

MUSLIM MANNERS

Muslim Tanzania is a relatively tolerant society. A disapproving glance rarely escalates to an actual admonishment. Still, in order not to embarrass yourself or offend others there are a few social rules worth respecting:

- First and foremost, do not use your left hand to pass or receive anything, or when shaking hands. (Its use in hygiene means the left hand is regarded as "unclean.")

- In traditional Muslim societies, like some neighborhoods of Zanzibar's Stonetown, it is offensive for men and, even more so, women to bare their knees or shoulders. Women travelers, especially on parts of the coast where tourists remain a novelty, should respect this rule.

- While some mosques exhibit spectacular architecture with enticing, shady courtyards, it is inappropriate to enter without first seeking an invitation. Often this is simply a matter of politely asking members congregated outside.

In keeping with Tanzania's religious tolerance, many practicing Muslims today blend Islam with traditional animist beliefs (see below). Muslim adherents may still consult faith healers and spiritualists in times of ill health or misfortune.

HOLIDAYS AND RELIGIOUS FESTIVALS

Most businesses are closed during public holidays, but festivities celebrating religious occasions can be colorful, flamboyant and well worth attending.

Ramadan

Ramadan, the ninth month of the Islamic year, is the hallmark festival of Islam and the largest celebration in Tanzania. This is the month in which the Koran was first revealed to the Prophet Mohammed by the angel Gabriel. Because the Muslim calendar is determined by the lunar cycle, Ramadan does not synchronize with the Western calendar; like all Islamic months it moves forward eleven days each solar year

Ramadan is a holy month set aside for prayers and purity. Muslims fast between the hours of

sunrise and sunset, and refrain from anything that may be considered a physical indulgence, such as eating, drinking, smoking, or sexual activity. Tempers can sometimes be short in the first days of Ramadan as adherents suffer their respective withdrawal symptoms. After the sun sets at the end of each day, families and friends gather together to break their fast. The twenty-seventh night, Laylat al-Qadr (the Night of Power) is the holiest night in the year, and devout believers practice retreat in a mosque. It is believed that on this night God determines the course of the world for the coming year.

During Ramadan, non-Muslims are expected to respect the sensibilities of their companions and not eat, drink, or smoke in public areas during the day. Many local restaurants will close during daylight hours, and those that stay open often screen tables from the view of the street.

Toward the end of the month, the anticipation becomes palpable. Muslims everywhere wait with bated breath for sight of the new moon, which signals the end of Ramadan.

Eid-ul-Fitr

The festivities of Eid-ul-Fitr are in celebration of the end of Ramadan. They are marked by prayers, feasting, the exchange of gifts, and the giving of alms. There are large and lively street parties in Muslim neighborhoods late into the night. Everyone dresses up in their finery and games are played by young and old alike.

Eid-ul-Adha

Two months after Eid-ul-Fitr comes Eid-ul-Adha (or Eid ul-Kebir), the feast of the sacrifice, commemorating Abraham's willingness to sacrifice his son. Muslims all over the world sacrifice an animal on this day. The occasion marks the end of the official Hajj, the annual pilgrimage to Mecca.

Eid ul-Maulid

Three months later is Eid ul-Maulid, a festival in honor of the Prophet's birthday.

Other Faiths

The usual Christian holidays such as Christmas and Easter are celebrated in Tanzania, as is Diwali, the colorful Hindu festival of lights. Hindu festivals are particularly noisy!

PUBLIC HOLIDAYS IN TANZANIA

New Year's Day	January 1
Zanzibar Revolution Day	January 12
Easter	March/April
Union Day	April 26
Labor Day	May 1
Eid ul-Maulid (Prophet's birthday)*	
Maonyesho ya Saba Saba (Peasants' Day)	July 7
Wakulima ya Nane Nane (Farmers' Day)	August 8
Mwalimu Julius Nyerere Day (climax of Uhuru Torch Race)	October 14
Ramadan begins*	
Eid ul-Fitr (end of Ramadan)*	
Eid ul-Adha / Eid ul-Kebir (Hajj date)*	
Independence Day	December 9
Christmas	December 25
Boxing Day	December 26

*Indicate Islamic holidays, which fall approximately eleven days earlier each year.

CHRISTIANITY

It is unclear when Christianity first arrived in Tanzania, though evidence points to the Portuguese ships piloted by the explorer Vasco da Gama in 1488. Whatever the case, it would be at least three hundred more years until it really began to take root, when the missionary influx into East Africa began in earnest. The highest concentration of Christians is in the northeast of Tanzania, around Moshi, which is where intensive missionary activity occurred, beginning in the mid-nineteenth century. Since then, Christianity is estimated to

have attracted a following of about 40 percent of the Tanzanian population. The country's Christians are composed mainly of Roman Catholics, Protestants, and Pentecostals. Today, Christians—individuals, groups, and missions—are an integral element of the Tanzanian social fabric.

Although the Tanzanian coast is hardly restricted to Muslims only, it is the interior that has a more Christian feel. This is likely the result of the numerous missions established throughout the country from the late 1800s onward. The fact that these missions raised money in the industrialized world and used it to buy the freedom of thousands of slaves may help to explain Christianity's rapid rise in popularity.

One of the most significant aspects of Tanzanian Christianity is the vibrant spirituality enjoyed at all levels. Sunday services tend to be very lengthy affairs and are geared as much to socializing and sharing news with friends and neighbors as to religion. Walk past a church on Sunday and it is possible for the visitor to enjoy one of the great musical performances of his or her stay in Tanzania. Local church choirs typically range in quality from outstanding to world-class: many raise the roof every weekend with rousing gospel. Boisterous, *bon vivant* Christianity is alive and well in Tanzania. It is a worthwhile cultural experience to drop by and see the engaging difference between a Tanzanian Sunday service and the more subdued atmosphere of mainstream Christian worship in, say, Europe.

Beyond Belief

A visitor's religious persuasion is often of great interest to Tanzanians. Atheists are almost unheard of in local culture, so claiming to be one sometimes causes genuine shock. To avoid lengthy debates on religion or the existence of God, it's best to steer clear of the subject.

TRADITIONAL AFRICAN BELIEFS AND CUSTOMS

Indigenous beliefs in Tanzania are typically animist and are often followed in conjunction with Christianity or Islam. Since long before the beginning of recorded history, Tanzanian traditional practices have focused on ancestor worship, the land, and various ritual objects.

There are many indigenous religions, which differ from tribe to tribe, but some generalities apply to all, among them the belief that the living stand between their ancestors and the unborn. Like many other traditional belief systems, those in Tanzania embrace natural phenomena—the rise and fall of the tides, the waxing and waning moon, rain and drought, and the rhythmic pattern of agriculture. Another common denominator is the belief in a Supreme Being, or Creator.

The Maasai worship Engai, a deity residing in a fiery volcanic crater near the Kenyan border and the source of all cattle. Until recently, private ownership was a foreign concept to the Maasai, who believed that every head of cattle in the world was theirs by godly decree. This often made life difficult for neighboring pastoralists, who were forced to fight for their livestock. Ongoing land and population pressures, however, along with new government policies, have tempered this Maasai tradition.

Over the centuries, the Maasai have perfected gaining maximum benefit from their herds. Since they have no value once dead, cattle are slaughtered for eating only on special occasions. In the meantime cows are periodically bled by puncturing an artery in the neck. The wound is then resealed and allowed to heal while the blood is mixed with milk for a drink that Maasai consider nutritious and delicious; it forms a significant component of their traditional diet.

The Boy on the Mountaintop

Ceremonial leaders in the Maasai tribe believe themselves to be descended from a boy with magical powers. According to legend, Maasai warriors found the young child naked and alone on a mountaintop. They chose to adopt him. They found that he had the power to make springs bubble up from the ground, grass grow, and pools of water appear. Even in times of famine, his cattle were always well fed and fat.

Mount Hanang, in the central Rift Valley, is the home of Aseeta, the God of the Datoga tribe, whose influence over day-to-day affairs is minimal, but who monitors them through his all-seeing eye, the sun.

Traditional healers and diviners are often consulted in times of illness or other adversity. Sorcery and witchcraft are also alive, though taboo, in Tanzania—as in much of Africa. Magic, both black and white, is controversial among Tanzanians. The educated, urban population denounces it as repugnant and primitive, while there is a large underground following in the countryside. A quick trip to the local art market will turn up numerous examples of magical masks and talismans. The newspapers frequently run stories of shamans, witch doctors, and magic, though the government condemns these beliefs and practices. Whether they actually believe in magic or not, Tanzanians certainly tend toward superstition.

WEDDINGS

Tanzanian weddings, whenever possible, are lavish affairs, at which sometimes more than one couple marry. Hundreds of friends and family members throng to church—in the case of Christians—to sing, clap, and watch the brides and grooms take their vows. Following the ceremony, it's time to celebrate.

Weddings are often so big, with family and friends numbering in the thousands, that a committee is formed to plan the event.

Weddings by Committee

Yes—every Tanzanian wedding has a committee of friends to solicit and spend contributions for the elaborate celebrations. Bad committees are notorious for spending the money on their own wining and dining while they discuss venues, music, and food. Good committees are rare.

Tira Shubart, "Marrying Faiths in Tanzania,"
BBC News

It is considered acceptable for families to go into debt in order to fund the finest wedding possible. But, to help ease their burden, families typically circulate an envelope for donations. In a sense, those wishing to attend the wedding buy their invitation. On the day of the ceremony, food, drinks, and live music are all included, and sometimes transportation to and from the event, a handy feature when the music and dancing continue into the early morning hours.

Gifts are expected and are typically delivered amid song and dance. Depending on the arrangements, a long conga-type line of gift-bearing well-wishers winds itself past the gift table, each person leaving behind a token of their goodwill until a small mountain of presents replaces what was once an item of folding garden furniture.

Muslim weddings differ from Christian ones in several respects, the most obvious being the absence of alcohol. Preparation of the bride is another unique feature that involves women of the groom's family—*kungwi*—undertaking a thorough cleansing of the bride. Once she has been lathered and scrubbed, henna is applied to the hands, the forearms, and feet. It is the only form of decoration allowed. According to tradition, even nail polish will render the pre-wedding cleansing process invalid. Incense is wafted over the bride, her clothes, and the couple-to-be's bedroom. The groom may not see the bride for the entire day before the ceremony but, after the vows are exchanged, the celebrations begin. Gifts are presented in the same manner as at a Christian wedding.

Tanzanian custom holds that women represent wealth to their families. The groom's family must compensate the bride's family for the loss of her, usually in the form of gifts or a symbolic sum of money to her parents, grandparents, brothers-in-law, and cousins.

MAKING FRIENDS

While Tanzanians place great importance on friendship, it is second in line to family. Friends are for socializing, sharing a beer, and telling stories; family is where Tanzanians turn in times of need. That line becomes blurred for longtime family intimates, who might, for instance, find themselves approached for work by the son of a close friend.

Attending local events such as weddings or funerals will help in building your social confidence. Volunteering on such occasions is a quick way to make friends and earn respect. Or, though it might feel awkward at first, asking a Tanzanian who lives nearby to act as a tourist guide for you is a good way to make a new friend. Tanzanians are proud of their country and like to show it off.

Some Tanzanians are so friendly it can be a bit alarming. They are relaxed, outgoing, and often intensely curious, and will approach a visitor just about anywhere: the bus ramp, the street corner, the bar. The result is an experience that is far removed from the brusque, no-nonsense interactions experienced in many Western urban centers. They are touchy-feely people and are likely to put a hand on your shoulder, or touch your hand and look in the general direction of your face during conversation.

Tanzanians are always ready to strike up a conversation. It sometimes leads to an invitation, lunch, or an offer to show a visitor around the city. Such fast and easy acquaintances sometimes go on to last a lifetime, or may be just a way to pass the time. But friendship can also bring with it expectations of favors, favoritism, or assistance. Given the low average income, people you know may decline an invitation to a social event if it is not clear that someone else is paying. Because of the social structure it is not considered shameful to expect to be "sponsored" by a friend or colleague. Tanzanians call this an "offer."

Other expectations might manifest themselves in the workplace. For instance, due to Tanzania's high rate of unemployment, most employees will expect a personal relationship or friendship to effect the hiring of friends and family, or at least bump them up toward the top of the list (see Chapter Eight).

GREETINGS

In the context of their laid-back disposition and sense of family ties and responsibility, Tanzanians also adhere to a strong social code. Emphasis is placed on manners and politeness—difficult to maintain when faced with aggressive solicitors and hustlers—and elaborate greetings are always expected.

Tanzanians value the moment of meeting, where two people catch up on recent events. It is important always to allow adequate time to do this with friends, colleagues, clients, and civil servants, as relationships are established through continued contact. Failure to go through the expected greetings routine can result in Tanzanians perceiving you as rude, thereby decreasing their desire for collaboration.

Typically, Tanzanians greet you with a handshake—sometimes this even applies to husband and wife—followed by inquiries into your well-being and that of your family, children, home, work, and even a discussion of the events of the past few days. Under normal circumstances this greeting will typically last between three and fifteen minutes.

It is considered impolite to launch straight into the subject of your business, even if you are just asking for directions from a bystander. With strangers, the absolute minimum is a routine consisting of *jambo* (Swahili for hello), *habari?* (how are you?), and *mzuri* (fine).

On the street, or in a more informal setting, you might say *mambo vipi?* (slang for how are you?—a bit like how's it going? or what's up?). The answer to this is *poa* (cool). Regardless of the reply this is typically followed by *hujambo?* (problems?), the reply *sijambo* (no problems) and finally *karibu* (welcome), then *asante sana* (thank you very much). When entering a home, it is customary to call out *hodi* and wait for the customary *karibu*.

HANDSHAKES

As with greetings, there is a choice of Tanzanian handshakes and they can be rather elaborate.

- The most simple and informal handshake, typical among young people, features "bumping fists." This is followed by tapping the thumb side of your clenched fist to your chest.

- The semiformal handshake, which can be used in almost every situation, involves the two opposing hands coming together, palms facing—identical to a traditional Western handshake. Then, in one smooth movement, the palms slide forward and up as each person briefly grasps the other's thumb in their fist. Then the hands slide back down to the original palms-facing handshake. While this handshake is the most common, letting a local take the lead will spare any awkwardness.

- The most formal handshake is that known worldwide: right hands grasping, palms facing. This is the version most often adopted in the upper tiers of business, government, and education.

- If your right hand is busy, wet, or dirty when a hand is offered, you are expected to proffer your wrist or any other part of your right arm in return.

Most visitors will find greetings involve additional questions regarding their place of origin, length of stay, and destination. You might have to respond endlessly to these standard questions, but it is worth remembering that such small talk is a great opportunity for a Tanzanian to practice their English or possibly for you both to spark up a new friendship. The best recipe here is a sense of humor, patience, and a smile.

Take it as a Compliment!

Interestingly, it is acceptable between Tanzanian women to comment on each other's weight gain. While this may be a sensitive subject in other cultures, in Africa being larger is a visual sign of success: it means they are eating well and enjoying free time. Should you be told in glowing terms that you have put on weight, while it may go against the grain, the appropriate response is simply to say "Thank you."

Regard for Age

Age is very important in Tanzanian culture and underpins an established societal structure. It determines social ranking in general and in the workplace, especially among women. The ages of two people meeting set the tone of the greetings. *Shikamoo* (I show my respect) is a greeting reserved for elders or people of stature within the community. It is typically followed by the title *babu* for an elderly man or *bibi* for an elderly woman.

A new employee who is younger than anyone else will often be addressed as *mtoto* (child), while an older woman might be called *mama* (mother). Younger employees may also be asked to do childish tasks, such as running errands.

INVITATIONS HOME

In more urban areas, where the cultural divide between the Tanzanian lifestyle and that of the developed world is no longer so vast, invitations home for lunch or dinner are more likely to happen.

If you are invited, you can expect a semiformal atmosphere where everyone in the household is in attendance and on their best behavior. This will wear off as the visit goes on, or in subsequent visits, but helps underscore the importance the family places on entertaining company. No matter the type of home, whatever the wealth or social standing of your hosts, they will make every effort to dress respectably for the occasion, and so should you as their guest. Most clothing is acceptable as long as it is not scruffy, though a collared or golf shirt or a blouse is preferable to a T-shirt. Jeans are acceptable at informal gatherings, though slacks are preferred.

Some Tanzanian households remove their shoes at the door to limit the dirt being tracked in. Others don't. If there are shoes left at the door, follow suit. If unsure, remove your shoes in the presence of your host. They will be quick to tell you otherwise, if that's the household policy.

For the vast majority of visitors, only a guided tour will make it possible to see inside the homes of some of Tanzania's pastoral people, such as the Maasai. This is also the case with the Hadzabe, one of the last hunter-gatherer societies left in Africa. Although they have no houses to speak of and sleep under the stars, theirs is a society well worth experiencing. Going on a specially arranged cultural tour into the homes of remote Africans might at first seem superficial, but is still highly recommended and far better than not having the opportunity at all.

Tanzanians take great pride in their food; they love making it and sharing it. The hostess — cooking and kitchen duties are almost universally performed by women—usually makes far more food than required, to ensure that everyone has enough to eat. The rule to remember is that, if your plate is clean, it means you are still hungry and the host will ensure more food arrives. It is considered polite when you've finished always to leave a little food on the plate. In non-Muslim households, beer, pop, or juice are typically served with meals and tea or coffee afterward.

When invited to lunch or dinner at a Tanzanian home, it is customary to bring a small token of appreciation. Alcohol is fine unless it is a Muslim household, in which case it is considered the height of bad manners. But flowers, spices, or anything sweet will be appreciated regardless of religious persuasion.

ATTITUDES TO FOREIGNERS

Foreigners gain immediate respect when they make an effort to learn and use Swahili. Tanzanians are particularly proud of their national language, since it is the lingua franca of the country and is not a remnant of European colonization. In general, Tanzanians appreciate this bequest from Julius Nyerere, whether or not they agree with his philosophy or his government.

Karibu is the word visitors will likely hear most often during their visit to Tanzania. Meaning welcome, it is a symbol of the warmth and openness of Tanzanian culture. Enter a home or place of business and the words *karibu sana* (very welcome) will probably be the first to greet you.

Haggling

After such a warm and pleasant greeting, it comes as a surprise to some visitors that they must haggle or bargain for a price they think is fair. This is particularly true when hiring a taxi or a

guide, organizing a trek or safari, or buying souvenirs and art. Though it may be easy to take offense at perceived overcharging by shopkeepers, understanding the system keeps things in perspective.

First, the opening price quoted is just that: an opener. The original quote might be high because experience shows that some visitors will pay the asking price to avoid haggling. Following the opening offer, however, the shopper is expected to make a counteroffer. This will go back and forth until a mutually agreeable price is reached.

While feeling that you have overpaid can be annoying, most visitors agree they are irritated more by the feeling of having been cheated than by the actual sum of money involved—which is usually a pittance. Considering the seller might be charging a few pennies more for a pile of fruit or a couple of dollars more for an art item in order simply to eat, it is worth, at the very least, erring on the side of generosity.

Bargaining in Tanzania probably dates back to the arrival of the Arab traders, or possibly earlier to the hunter-gatherer societies. Whatever the case, today it is a way to socialize, to slow down a transaction, and chat. Bargaining is an excuse for interaction; understanding this is key to carrying it out successfully.

Avoid shopping in a hurry because trying to rush through a purchase will almost certainly end in a higher price. Time must be taken to chat, counteroffer, chat some more, and counteroffer again.

No-Haggle Zones
Established supermarkets are one of the few places where bargaining is not done. Restaurants and bars, too, have fixed prices on their menus.

Shopping in Tanzania sometimes seems to deserve as a motto the Latin expression *caveat emptor*, or "let the buyer beware." Thoroughly check the product you are purchasing and count your change. Most business transactions are straightforward but occasionally integrity is overwhelmed by the poverty of the seller.

Coping with Begging
In Tanzania begging takes many forms. Requests for money come from all directions—from well-dressed, able-bodied young men to the severely disabled. The perception that foreigners are wealthy makes them the targets of frequent financial demands.

Perhaps in part because of *undugu*, there's never a wrong time to ask someone for a donation or a little money for food or family. It might, rather surprisingly, come from the restaurant waiter before the meal comes or from the maintenance manager at the hotel. It might simply happen in the middle of a busy intersection, while waiting for the lights to change. How you react depends on personal preference, but even the most philanthropic will likely eventually balk at the relentlessly repeated "give me money" that follows foreigners down the streets and through the markets of many towns and villages. Some blame years of aid and donations being distributed by wealthy first-world countries for instilling a sense of expectation.

Many native Africans give to the genuinely needy (who are sometimes difficult to discern) when they have the money. If not, it's simply a matter of saying "no."

ROMANCE AND THE VISITOR

Lean, muscular, and exotic, Tanzanians are frequently beautiful people. In urban centers, especially in nightclubs and bars, women often wear outline-flattering or shoulder-revealing garments; men like to wear cologne and fancy shirts. Yet dating in Tanzania differs considerably from European and American customs—hand-holding is very rarely seen and kissing in public is almost unheard of.

The visitor looking for love in Tanzania should also take a few other things into account.

Perhaps because of a perception that they are unattainable, Western women are particularly desirable to many Tanzanian men. An attractive single woman can and will gather a formidable following of potential suitors, some of whom bluntly suggest marriage. Such proposals speak to the motivations of Tanzanians in search of intercultural relationships. Hollywood films and other media feed stereotypes of Western men and women with exaggerated perceptions of wealth. These spur-of-the-moment propositions are driven by visions of a life of ease, rather than serious matrimonial considerations.

In contrast, Tanzanian women tend to be much less aggressive than their Western counterparts, shy even, so, typically, fending off unwanted female advances is not a problem for male visitors. Foreign men may be seen as something of a novelty or, more pragmatically, as an appealing meal ticket.

Tanzanian attitudes to male–female relationships are basically patriarchal. Tanzanian men can sometimes be unusually possessive and often demand the highest level of loyalty. Yet these very same men regard it as acceptable to have mistresses, who are referred to colloquially as *nyumba ndogo* ("little house"). A man's wife and first family constitute his primary residence, but many Tanzanian men also support another woman and sometimes her children. Such liaisons are much more than just one-night stands to satisfy physical desire. Rather, the other family is thought of as a man's secondary residence, hence the term "little house."

This is an excellent example of how Tanzanian urbanites have created hybrid conceptions of morality and codes for responsible conduct within romantic relationships, drawing on both African and European ideals.

A Western man or woman embarking on a romantic relationship with a Tanzanian while in the country should expect that there will be more pressure on the foreigner to adjust to local custom than the other way around. Despite different traditions, relationships between Tanzanians and visitors are relatively common as a broad spectrum of potential partners are available.

Though arranged marriages do still occur, today the younger generation is often free to marry for love alone, especially in urban areas. Most tribal traditions also allow men to marry more than one wife if they so wish, although this has become less common with changing attitudes. Even Muslims, whose Islamic faith permits polygamy, often settle for a one-wife family.

Cash Conquers All

Love is also a purchasable commodity in Tanzania. Where poverty is pervasive, money can make unattractive people good-looking. This helps explain beautiful young Tanzanians dating older, overweight foreigners.

Sexual Russian Roulette

Once a certain death sentence, in the West HIV/AIDS is now largely controlled by antiretroviral medication. Most Africans cannot afford these drugs, however, and HIV/AIDS is alive and thriving in Tanzania, as in much of sub-Saharan Africa. With one in ten citizens

HIV positive, sexual promiscuity in Tanzania is a form of Russian roulette. Especially when unprotected. To make matters worse, anti-safe-sex information abounds: some officials blame condoms for ruining marriages and declare their use as ineffectual in halting the disease's advance. A particularly disturbing, and surprisingly widely believed myth is that having unprotected sex with a virgin cures AIDS.

chapter five

THE TANZANIANS AT HOME

THE HOUSEHOLD

With so many different lifestyles and standards of living, Tanzanian households come in all shapes and sizes: from huts made of sticks and mud to

urban high-rise apartments and luxurious houses amidst sprawling grounds. Most are designed to be cool when it is hot, dry during the rainy seasons, and secured against thieves. It is this last feature that makes urban Tanzanian homes stand out most from their European, North American, and Asian counterparts. Heavy steel bars on the windows (even in high-rise apartments), along with high gates and fences, bolts and padlocks, security guards, and, in the case of the wealthy, alarms, attest to the Tanzanians' emphasis on security and the protection of their belongings.

Due in part to the development of informal neighborhoods and slums, Tanzanians do not use addresses in the usual sense. As a result, properties are sometimes identified by plot numbers used by the municipality for zoning and division purposes. More commonly, finding a particular residence or business involves following directions that work back from the nearest major landmark. This makes postal delivery impossible, so those who receive mail must pay for a PO box at the local post office.

By virtue of economic circumstance, urban and rural architecture is often no-frills. To keep homes cool, floors are often bare concrete or tile, likewise the walls. Corrugated roofs reflect the sun's heat, while overhangs and landscaping provide shade.

In the bush, rural Tanzanians typically build simple homes of sticks and brush—often circular—and cover them with thatch roofs. Most of these homes have fenced-in areas secured by thorny branches to protect the livestock from

predators at night. There is no plumbing or electricity: toilets are placed outside and are little more than a deep hole in the ground, with a small barrier for privacy. Despite their simplicity, these homes are the pride and joy of their owners. Every day the women sweep the mud floors with brooms of twigs and twine. Kitchen fires burn at all hours; children play outside; chickens scratch the dirt; and a dog or two lies in the shade.

From a completely different cultural source,

and a truly exotic one at that, is Zanzibari architecture. It dates back to the time of the sultans, who brought designs with them from the deserts of Oman. These buildings, with their rooftop terraces and flat roofs, ornate latticework and cool shady courtyards—as well as their incredible doors—draw visitors from around the world. Unfortunately, they are not suited to the monsoon rains of Zanzibar and structures that have not been restored in recent years are in an advanced state of decay.

Interior decoration of homes directly reflects the income of their occupants, from spartan to opulent. Many people have no power or running water, have never owned a television, nor the simplest things most visitors take for granted, such as curtains over the windows. Many homes and most businesses do display a large picture of the current president. This is typically mounted high on the wall and looks down upon the family or the shopkeeper and his customers, speaking volumes about Tanzanian deference to "the big man."

Those who can afford it invest in a television. But even those who cannot are not left out during essential programming. For instance, during the all-important televised Africa Cup of Nations soccer tournament, televisions are placed in windows, bars, and sometimes street corners, where huge crowds gather round to follow the action. Videocassette recorders are still common, but the DVD is quickly surpassing them in popularity and availability. Most urban neighborhoods have DVD rental shops, though they are less common in the suburbs.

FEMALE ROLES

Under Tanzania's statutory law, women and men are equal. Under the country's other coexisting legal systems, however, customary law (according to the tribe), Indian law (for people of Indian descent), and Islamic sharia law (for Muslims), women are subordinated to men.

Girls are withdrawn from school before boys when money becomes tight or they are needed to work at home. Marriages are often arranged and dowries are paid by the groom's family, ensuring that for poorer families finances are sometimes the only criteria for suitability. Wives are then expected to stay and make the home, raise the children, clean and cook, and, at the same time, even work.

To keep women from exercising power they are sometimes excluded from family decision-making

processes and forbidden from being seen in public life. Laws exist to protect women against gender-based violence, but these are feeble and difficult to enforce. If a woman does not seek assistance it is unlikely that help will find her. Statistics show that incidents of violence against women are common and increasing annually.

While this paints an extremely depressing picture of the plight of Tanzanian women, times are changing. The government has launched a campaign of education and enforcement to curb female circumcision (see Chapter Two) and has denounced domestic violence.

While the husband is still king of his castle and head of the family, women are striving for more equality. If letters and editorials in daily newspapers are anything to go by, the national consciousness seems to be awakening to the fact that women deserve better.

DOMESTIC STAFF

In Tanzania, employing domestic staff is common for anyone who can afford them. Security guards, gardeners, cooks, and cleaners tend to the homes of the middle class and privileged. The work is unskilled, yet not dangerous, making it popular for women and the elderly. Perhaps because the job is viewed as being relatively simple, wages are typically low, though workers must sometimes use them to support extended family, in addition to feeding, housing, and clothing themselves.

STANDARDS OF LIVING

For the vast majority of Tanzanians living standards are desperately poor. As recently as the mid-1990s, estimates were that 41 percent of the population were undernourished. Tanzania continues to have rising inflation and declining standards of living. More recent studies reveal that 36 percent of Tanzanians still live below the poverty line, yet the price of staples, such as rice and corn, has surged in the first decade of the new millennium.

Most Tanzanians spend what little money they earn on basic necessities: food, rent, clothing, fuel, and transportation. There is little left over for entertainment and recreation, which are considered luxuries.

Yet, despite this gloomy reality, Tanzanians go about their daily lives stoically. They take pride in their appearance and the morning commute is usually a rush of immaculate and neatly pressed white shirts, blouses, and business attire. Traffic is thick during morning and evening rush hours, though brand-new vehicles are relatively rare. Tanzania's cars are all imported, most from China and Japan, and it is possible sometimes to see old Russian and Indian trucks grinding along, remnants of a bygone era.

DAILY LIFE

Early morning is popular with Tanzanians, who exercise or work before the heat of the day. The

lack of electricity in rural areas ensures early nights, shortly after the sun sets. As a result, rural folk tend to rise before the sun does. In urban areas, the call to prayer at the mosques means that most people are up around 5:00 a.m. Most Tanzanians breakfast at home; many grab a bite on their way to work. The commute is by bicycle, public transportation, or car.

Grocery shopping in Tanzania is generally done in the markets. These noisy, open-air affairs are overflowing with life as wives, cooks, and other domestic help haggle for the day's supplies. It is here they buy live chickens, fish, eggs, fresh produce, household goods, and every imaginable necessity. What's on sale also tends to be the cheapest.

Those who want a less hectic shopping experience, imported foods, and fixed prices— and who can afford it—shop at any of the growing number of supermarkets around the country. Some of these are truly outstanding, but their prices can be even higher than in the developed world.

Most Tanzanians who can afford it eat three meals a day. Lunch is the most popular meal to eat out. Some larger companies and government agencies have cafeterias where simple, inexpensive meals are served. At others, employees simply go out to the nearest food stall. Those in the agriculture sector and with low-income jobs take lunch where they can, if they have it at all.

GROWING UP IN TANZANIA

Tanzanians love their children. Yet treasured and adored as they are, Tanzanian children are not spoiled. Most child rearing is modeled on the "seen and not heard" and "speak when spoken to" school of upbringing, which produces well-mannered, soft-spoken children who regard their elders with respect. Bad behavior is rare and you are unlikely to hear children screaming or throwing tantrums in a public place. Such behavior is not tolerated.

The complexities of modern Tanzanian households mean that children are often raised in various environments by mothers, nannies, grandmothers, aunts, and anyone else considered responsible. As a result, they grow up addressing any caring adult as "uncle" or "auntie."

Tanzanian children are taught from a young age the skills needed to contribute to the family and to the community. Girls begin learning how to do domestic chores and become "little mothers" to their younger siblings, while boys are proud to take on the very serious tasks of herding the goats and sheep or helping in the fields.

Because many children are brought up in poor homes they are acutely aware of the value of food, money, and possessions. This makes them all the more appreciative of anything they are given, be it a stick of chewing gum or hand-me-down clothing. Shoes are a real luxury, especially when school is several hours' walk away.

In a life devoid of television and video games, children entertain themselves by creating soccer balls from bundles of plastic, homemade cars from bottle caps (for wheels) and old wire, and dolls from pieces of stuffing and spare fabric.

EDUCATION

School is voluntary in Tanzania and is viewed with great respect by children and parents alike. It is the passport to a better future and taken very seriously.

Nyerere placed great importance on education. He made primary education compulsory and funded the building of village schools. The result was that, by the late 1980s, Tanzania's literacy rate was one of the highest in Africa. But, following

Nyerere's failed Ujamaa policies, government funding of primary schools ended. The new fees made school an impossible luxury for the poorest children and school enrollment quickly plummeted.

Those who could not afford school were sent into the workforce at a young age. Some estimates indicate that in Tanzania more than 450,000 children under the age of fifteen are working, some 30,000 of whom are employed in mines and on plantations where the work is considered dangerous.

Sadly, more than one-quarter of Tanzanians still do not complete primary school and a corresponding number can neither read nor write. The good news is that these statistics have improved dramatically in the past fifteen years and will hopefully continue to do so.

Although primary school is still free and 85 percent of children enroll, only about 65 percent graduate and, of them, just 5 percent complete their secondary education. There are a number of reasons for this low proportion: a lack of properly trained teachers, annual fees of 80,000/-, and a

shortage of schools all contribute.

In certain cultures, particularly among the more rural tribes, it is considered unnecessary to educate female children, many of whom are destined for an arranged marriage when they reach puberty.

TIME OUT

Leisure time is very important to Tanzanians.
In fact, it is probably the most important element
of their lives. Whether it's sitting in the park at
lunchtime, going out for a beer, or simply playing
a traditional Bao board game, Tanzanians are big
on relaxation.

Tanzania today is a place where life is kept
simple by economic necessity: many people do
not have the luxuries of mobile phones, Internet
access, PlayStations, iPods, television, or even the
ability to read. Instead they find ways to occupy
their spare time and keep themselves entertained
the old-fashioned way: women gather in the
shade of a tree to braid each other's hair; men

congregate around games of checkers played on homemade boards with bottle caps as pieces. Others sit on the front stoop, listening to the soccer game on a transistor radio or deep in debate with friends or neighbors.

SOCIAL EVENTS AND CELEBRATIONS

Church is among the biggest social events of the week. Some say the main reason they attend, particularly on Sundays, is because church provides a means of meeting regularly with neighbors and people from other villages. It is also a chance to dress up in one's best clothes and get away from the house and the daily grind of chores. Visitors are always welcome to join in the proceedings and doing so could lead to making connections within the community.

Likewise, market day is treated very much as a social event, as is soccer (which in Tanzania is called football).

Come vacation time, statistics indicate that many of those who can afford it head abroad. Families sometimes explore one of the country's national parks to view the wildlife. But, for the vast majority, where travel is simply an unaffordable luxury, what constitutes vacations are the colorful traditional celebrations and the usual singing, dancing, feasting, and drumming that go with all East African festivals. These are great events through which to absorb the Tanzanian culture and are highly recommended.

ZANZIBAR INTERNATIONAL FILM FESTIVAL

Also known as the Festival of the Dhow Countries, this spans two weeks at the end of June and beginning of July. ZIFF has a reputation as the largest annual cultural event in East Africa and is one of the top ten festivals on the continent.

Each year this festival showcases upward of one hundred films, a three-day literary forum, a Children's Panorama—in which some 200,000 children participate—and exhibitions that highlight women in the arts.

Other big festivals are worth attending as exhibitions of Tanzanian spirit and culture.

Marriages, graduation, birthdays, New Year, Eid-ul-Fitr, football victories—the list of reasons Tanzanians celebrate is extensive. The best events, however, are the small ones that are not announced everywhere. These might include being invited to a wedding in a small town or to another rite-of-passage celebration. Getting away from the tourist haunts and into the villages, mingling with Tanzanians, is the most effective way to learn about life in out-of-the-way places.

TANZANIAN FOOD

Tanzania's national dish is called *ugali*—though to be accurate it's not a dish so much as a staple similar to rice or potatoes. This mixture of maize, flour, and water can range from a porridgelike substance to a doughlike ball and to unaccustomed palates it tastes rather like cardboard. But it is a cheap source of carbohydrates and is therefore eaten by the poorest people from one end of the country to the other. When served in the consistency of mashed potatoes, *ugali* can be dipped into a stew, which usually contains vegetables and occasionally meat.

Ugali aside, the real national dish is more likely Chips Mayai. This is basically a french fries omelet that provides substance, flavor, and some nutrition, which helps explain its popularity.

On the street, Chips Mayai has to fight for its place in the lineup of national dishes against another local favorite: chicken (called *kuku*)—usually a well-roasted drumstick and thigh with delicious crispy skin——plus boiled spinach, a thin but tasty tomato-based gravy (sauce), and french fries, rice, chapati (Indian bread), or *ugali*. This favorite local meal, which, like most traditional dishes, tends to be mildly spicy, is traditionally eaten with the right hand. Cutlery, however, almost always accompanies the plate when it arrives. *Ugali*, in particular, is best pulled apart by hand and used like a sponge to mop up gravy.

Tanzanian dishes are usually simple and most frequently made with chicken, goat, or beef, with more fish featured along the coast. (The cuisine rarely caters to the vegetarian palate, though rice, beans, and perhaps spinach and similar vegetables are available almost everywhere.) Traditional meals tend to be accompanied by sauces, stews, and curries. If anything, goat is more popular than beef, in part because goats do not often spend their lives pulling heavy loads. As a result, the meat is usually more tender and filled with flavor. In contrast, Tanzanian cows are beasts of burden, so the beef can be chewy.

Because many meats are bought and sold in markets, where the heat and a lack of refrigeration sometimes render sanitary conditions questionable, meals tend toward being slightly overcooked. Fish is no exception, but is usually delicious anyway. *Pili Pili*, a spicy local red pepper sauce, is often used to heighten flavor in a variety of dishes, especially seafood and curries.

EATING OUT

Eating out in Tanzania is often easier and cheaper than eating in. There are restaurants for just about every taste and budget. Most of them are very good and even the least expensive, those that cater

to low-income Tanzanians, tend to serve food that is simple but tasty. Well-to-do Tanzanians might frequent restaurants that are known for their atmosphere as well as their food. Their less fortunate fellow citizens are more likely to aim for good food and eat it in whatever the ambience happens to be.

Dishes range in price from less than a US dollar to the very reasonable, though expect to pay more for Western dishes, or in restaurants serving exotic foreign food. That said, many of these restaurants are still considerably less expensive than their Western equivalents and indulging in the predictable flavors of your native land is a tempting option for the homesick. But  for some this would still be an unnecessary expense in the face of so much reasonably priced and delicious local food.

Western food, in the form of club sandwiches and fancy salads, poached eggs and pizza, is available in the bigger cities, but only in a few select restaurants and international hotels. Asian food has also made strong inroads into Tanzanian culture. The spices of Zanzibar are put to good use in Indian food, which is renowned in many areas of the country. It's worth making it a priority to dine at least once in an Indian restaurant, especially in Dar es Salaam, which has a large Indian population and culinary delights to match. The curries are inexpensive and simply delicious. The big cities also have a smattering of

Thai, Chinese, Italian, Ethiopian, and Japanese restaurants that are worthwhile trying for something different.

Fast food, Western-style, has won the hearts of Tanzanians who can afford it but is an unaffordable luxury for many. The burger-and-fries staples of more developed countries have begun to catch on, though the big multinational fast-food chains have yet to make inroads here. Instead, it's fast food Tanzanian style. This can be worth exploring as some of it is cheap and delicious, and lacks the highly processed nature of that in the West.

Gourmet Stonetown

While there is a degree of predictability in local food across the country, assumptions can be thrown out the window in Zanzibar. In particular, the island's capital city, Stonetown, is home to numerous restaurants that serve some of the finest cuisine in the country, some of them at the most reasonable prices. Seafood is at its freshest here and is usually the best bet from the menu.

The night market at Stonetown's Forodhani Gardens is rated as one of the best street-stall food markets in Africa. Delicious and inexpensive, all manner of food can be sampled here.

Eating in restaurants and on the street in Tanzania is a fairly safe option. But sensitive stomachs might react to the exotic spices and cleanliness is also sometimes an issue. Ensure that food, especially meat, is cooked thoroughly to ensure a trouble-free holiday.

Eating Etiquette

Tanzania is very laid-back and table manners are fairly relaxed. Of course, the higher a person ascends the social hierarchy, the greater the expectation of refinement. Many of Tanzania's most influential figures are Western educated and so have imported Western table manners. But, in general, the idiosyncrasies of visitors' habits are likely to cause amusement rather than outright offense.

That said, the most important point of etiquette (especially at a Muslim table) is to use the right hand for eating and to refrain from eating or passing food with the left hand. If everyone else is eating with their fingers, it is best to do the same, even where cutlery is provided. Most Tanzanians eat in this way and washing your hands before and after the meal is normal.

It is considered polite to leave a little food on the plate at the end of the meal to show your hosts you are sated. If you are invited to eat but are not hungry, it is acceptable to explain you have just eaten. But eating a couple of mouthfuls anyway acknowledges the bond with your hosts.

TIPPING

- Tipping is expected in fancy and foreign restaurants, but is not mandatory, as in North America. Check if the gratuity has already been included on the bill. If not, and the service was good, 10 percent of the total is an acceptable tip.
- In local restaurants tips are also appreciated, though no more than 5 to 10 percent is expected.
- Waitresses especially appreciate tipping, though they are unlikely to become disgruntled if you don't.
- More generally, gratuities should not be confused with paying for a service. If a taxi driver delivers his passengers on time and safely, a small tip, usually just a few cents, is polite. Not leaving this money is unlikely to ruffle feathers. But car park attendants offer a service. They not only ensure you do not get a ticket; they also keep an eye on the car to make sure it is not broken into or stolen. Not leaving a token of your appreciation is frowned upon here. Tanzanians aren't shy to let foreigners know when they think they deserve a few extra shillings.

DRINKING

Tanzania is a nation that enjoys a drink. Consumption of alcohol is more prevalent in the north than in the coastal regions, where more Muslims are concentrated. Alcohol is readily available everywhere and there always seems to be someone who's up for a beer.

Before the government removed decades-old state controls and privatized beverage companies, having a beer with friends often meant standing in line for hours. And even then you weren't guaranteed a drink. These days it's much easier. Alcohol is sold in bars, restaurants, and supermarkets, and of course in shops dedicated to it.

The selection ranges from well-known imported brands to the cheapest local concoctions, with a good percentage of the population indulging in maize beer and other forms of home brew.

Konyagi

Konyagi is a popular local spirit in the gin category. In truth, it tastes like a cross between gin and tequila and is sold in all sizes from snip-top, double-shot sealed plastic baggies to hip flasks and 26 oz (768 ml) bottles.

Beer is relatively inexpensive and comes in many types, both locally brewed and imported from neighboring countries like Kenya and Uganda, and from the West. Local beer is normally sold in large, 16 fl oz (500 ml) bottles.

Municipal water is best avoided unless your stomach is used to it. Bottled water is available almost everywhere, even—to some degree—in most rural areas. (If you're venturing into the bush, it's better to take a purification system.) Ice is relatively rare: steer clear of it unless you're certain it's been made with purified water.

BARS AND NIGHTCLUBS

The pulse of Tanzania's nightlife is not just healthy, it's throbbing. Nightclubbing is alive and very popular in larger towns. Cities have dozens of nightclubs, while towns might have just one. Bars are ubiquitous, found in most hotels and on street corners across the country. Lines for nightclubs and bars are rare. They might occasionally occur in Dar es Salaam or Arusha but are almost unheard of elsewhere.

On the sartorial front, nothing more formal than jeans and a smart shirt is required, even at the fanciest hotel clubs and bars, though at these upscale venues elegance won't be out of place either. Most local bars and nightclubs have no dress code whatsoever, though a shirt is compulsory. The exception to this rule is when drinking at beach bars and clubs, especially on Zanzibar.

Though most towns and every city will have a few bars and clubs that are considered "rough," the vast majority are friendly places with a good atmosphere. Reputable establishments will almost always have at least one doorman, sometimes several, to keep the peace, though violence is far less an issue than petty thievery. Keep your valuables safely in your pockets and never leave mobile phones, wallets, or money sitting on the table.

Place Your Bets

Gambling is very common and becoming increasingly so among the well-to-do. Texas Holdem poker is gaining popularity in Tanzania as quickly as in the rest of the world. Casinos are springing up in the bigger cities and are as flashy as any Western equivalent. Although gambling is forbidden in Islam, some Muslims do gamble. They are, however, a tiny minority.

MUSIC AND DANCING

Music is a fundamental part of Tanzanian life, and concerts, both formal and impromptu, are numerous. Venues range from arts colleges and nightclubs to street corners and churches, featuring modern music with typically reggae, gospel, or hip-hop and rap origins. Blues and jazz, as well as tribal roots, are also hallmarks of Tanzanian music.

Taarab music is prominent in Tanzania, a culmination of a variety of musical influences from the country's past, including those from East Asia, sub-Saharan Africa, North Africa, the Middle East, and Europe. It's probably most prominent on Zanzibar, often played by a full Arab orchestra of violins, guitars, lutes, mandolins, harmoniums, and organs. It may not appeal to everyone's musical taste, but few will deny its appeal when played on a traditional dhow at sunset.

It is almost impossible not to hear the local music: it is played at full volume on the public transportation, and emanates from bars and restaurants, radios, and everywhere. It is a significant component of the Tanzanian identity.

And so is dancing. Tanzanians love to cut a rug and any opportunity will do. In addition to discos and concerts, dance features strongly at all the major social events, such as weddings, parties, and religious gatherings.

For those with a love of music, one of the signature events on Zanzibar is the Sauti za Busara music festival. Meaning Sounds of Wisdom, this is an international festival celebrating African music and takes place in February each year. It's here you'll hear music from far and wide on the continent.

SMOKING AND DRUGS

Smoking in Tanzania is inexpensive and the quality of cigarettes typically good. Apart from locally manufactured cigarettes there are also a number of imported brands available. Though cigarettes are reasonably priced, smoking remains a bit of a luxury. It is not as popular as elsewhere, nor is it banned in public places.

While a number of Tanzanians do smoke cigarettes, especially along the coast many prefer the flavorful hookah pipe, which has its roots in the Middle East and is particularly popular among those of Arab or similar descent. Tobacco sits in a clay bowl atop the pipe and the smoke is drawn down through water and eventually through long hoses to the smoker. The tobacco comes in a variety of flavors. What makes this type of smoking sociable is the number of people who can smoke the pipe at once, often sitting around a table and chatting. A single pipe may have as many as four hoses, or as few as just one, but you will not be expected to share hoses or mouthpieces with anyone else.

Drugs, of the recreational variety, are illegal in Tanzania. There are many young Tanzanians who enjoy smoking marijuana, but the penalties for possession or trafficking can be severe. Drugs such as cocaine and heroin are gradually gaining popularity, but are more prevalent in the port cities along the coast. Drug taking in Tanzania is just not recommended.

SHOPPING

Consumerism is not part of Tanzanian culture to the extent that it is elsewhere. There just aren't enough affluent consumers to sustain it. Shopping is more utilitarian, so to speak, and less about catering to the consumer's every desire.

Rather than shopping malls lined with Gucci boutiques and Rolex franchises, in Tanzania the main streets are full of foreign exchange bureaus and stores selling useful items like appliances, motorcycles, and stationery. It's worth noting, for example, that the only way to buy a good quality digital camera in Tanzania is to order it from overseas.

That said, Tanzania's bigger cities sell most things that are available in the developed world—a visitor just needs to know where to look. In particular, communities favored by expatriates are generally endowed with Western-style supermarkets, fresh bakeries, and boutique shopping (albeit limited).

There is a long tradition of craftsmanship in the country. Zanzibar's famous chests are breathtaking: made of rich local woods, sometimes with elaborate carving and brass or bone inlays. Other crafts, too, are appealing and unique to Tanzania.

While the economy is one of the poorest in the world, Tanzania is not necessarily home to the world's greatest bargains. Import duties and taxes ensure that most imported goods—from cereals to computers—are more expensive than elsewhere, though great deals can be had on locally produced goods, including art.

THEATER AND CINEMA

Tanzanian theater and dance are usually intertwined; a performance includes both elements. With their beating drums and traditional outfits, theater and dance typically act as windows to a tribal past and are most often far removed from Broadway's ostentatious sets and Shakespearean twists of plot.

Most tourist hotels host nightly dance displays. Usually the dancers come from the local community and perform their own tribal routines. Performance venues are typically outside, and often involve audience participation at some level, which can be difficult to refuse.

Tanzania's college of the performing arts, called Chuo Cha Sanaa, is the only one of its kind in East and Central Africa. Located in Bagamoyo, it acts as a barometer for music, dance, theater, and fine arts. The college's new indoor theater and concert hall are convenient during the rainy season, but the outdoor amphitheater is a great place to lounge in the shade and watch free performances most evenings. If arts and culture are your thing, time your visit to Bagamoyo with the end of September or beginning of October, when every year the college is home to the International Bagamoyo Arts Festival.

In Tanzania cinema (in movie theaters, rather than on DVD) is surprisingly scarce. For instance, the estimated four million residents of Dar es Salaam have just three movie theaters to choose from, one of which is dedicated to Bollywood features, the other two geared more toward Hollywood releases. Action adventure, with its attendant explosions and bullets flying everywhere, is far and away the most popular genre.

Seeing films is relatively expensive, which keeps crowds down. Those in the mood for something more cerebral or artistic should keep an ear to the ground as

some embassies and expatriate clubs host art house cinema nights.

THE ARTS

Tanzania has a flourishing arts scene. It is the birthplace of Tinga Tinga, an abstract, cartoonlike artistic style that has become popular with Tanzanians and visitors alike due to its humor and color. It is the most common type of painting at the countless roadside and market art stalls, though high quality is a little harder to find.

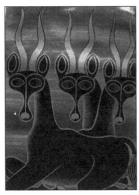

Just about every city and many towns have an art "district." This is typically an informal gathering of artists and art vendors who have opened a number of shops in close proximity. One of the largest such districts is Dar es Salaam's Mwenge Carvers' Market. As the name implies, carving is the specialty here, but the scores of stalls feature just about every art form, including a broad selection of paintings. Such markets benefit from their variety and competition leads to good prices.

Those who want to fully explore art in Tanzania should head to Bagamoyo, about 40 miles (60 km) north of Dar es Salaam. As we have seen, this is the home of Chuo Cha Sanaa, the heartbeat of the arts in East and Central Africa. This small college is at the cutting edge of artistic trends and is producing some of the best artists in the nation.

SPORTS

Soccer (called football) has an almost religious following in Tanzania, both at the national level and in Europe's Premier and Champions Leagues. Overseas games are followed closely, the Africa Cup of Nations fervently. Every two years this cup tournament pits the best teams from a dozen African countries against each other. Large crowds gather wherever there's a television and turnout at the matches is huge.

Fans are rowdy and boisterous at intermunicipal matches and their passions escalate in intensity at the national level. If there's a game on, it's an experience that should not be missed, though going in a group is recommended.

Most ardent soccer fans are young men between fourteen and thirty-five: when they're not yelling support for their soccer heroes, they're out on the field themselves, kicking around the day's best substitute for a ball. Soccer balls are relatively scarce in Tanzania, so it is common to see children—and sometimes young men—kicking around homemade balls made of rolled up bits of newspaper and old plastic bags. This they do in their bare feet and rare is the game where the locals aren't keen to show the visitor a thing or two. Kick off your shoes and learn soccer Tanzania style.

Given the former colony's exposure to British influence, and considering its population of South

Asians, it's a wonder cricket isn't bigger in Tanzania. But, like basketball and rugby, appropriate facilities are lacking and there is not a lot of time left over for recreation at the end of the working day.

WILDLIFE AND BIG GAME

Once prime hunting grounds for Tanzania's earliest inhabitants, the national parks and reserves now enjoy blanket protection and attract some 750,000 tourists a year. To the locals, these areas of wilderness conservation are a mixed blessing. On the one hand tourism employs some 30,000 Tanzanians. On the other, setting up the parks and reserves forced the people who once occupied that land to the fringes. The parks reduced available agricultural land and put a sudden end to ancient pursuits like hunting, collecting timber, and gathering medicinal herbs. What's more, farmers and pastoralists on the fringes are forbidden from using lethal force against wandering wildlife in defense of livestock and crops. This combination of effects has led to

poverty in the villages bordering the parks and, consequently, increased poaching.

The result is that the Tanzanian government makes ongoing efforts to ensure that locals benefit from money raised by the reserves, and are provided with employment and even meat from culled animals.

Wildlife is one of the main motivations for visiting Tanzania. People want the image of a cheetah silhouetted by a fiery red sunset seared in their minds or on film; or the earthquaking trumpet of a cantankerous bull elephant etched in their memories; or maybe just the sight of a yawning hippopotamus, its cavernous mouth baring a single, yellowed tooth the size of a man's fist. Whatever your expectations of wildlife in Africa, Tanzania will almost certainly surpass them.

The country has one of the highest proportions of parkland of any country in the world: about 35 percent is protected in some way or another and is home to some of nature's great wonders. Here is where the wildebeests pass through by the million on their annual migration, along with a half-million zebras—all of which are pursued by lions, leopards, cheetahs, hyenas, and vultures.

WHEN HISTORY AND FUTURE COLLIDE

The transition has been long underway, but members of the dwindling Hadzabe tribe, who now number fewer than 1,500, say they are being unduly hastened by a United Arab Emirates royal family, which plans to use the tribal hunting land as a personal safari playground.

The deal between the Tanzanian government and Tanzania UAE Safaris Ltd. leases nearly 2,500 sq. miles of this sprawling, yellow-green valley near the storied Serengeti Plain to members of the royal family, who chose it after a helicopter tour.

A Tanzanian official said that a nearby hunting area the family shared with relatives had become "too crowded" and that a member of the Abu Dhabi royal family "indicated that it was inconvenient" and requested his own parcel.

Stephanie McCrummen, Washington Post Foreign Service, June 10, 2007

The big five (lions, rhinoceroses, elephants, leopards and buffalo) also make their homes here.

Going on safari (the word means literally "to travel") into the Tanzanian bush can be a spellbinding adventure. With a good guiding outfit, and more importantly a good guide, an expedition to one of the country's national parks is the highlight of most people's stay.

Arusha is the closest city to Lake Manyara, the Ngorongoro Crater and the Serengeti, though seeing all three is best done in a week, as reaching the Serengeti alone is a full day's drive. Arusha National Park is the best bet for a day trip and provides awesome views of towering Mount Kilimanjaro.

From Dar es Salaam, Sadaani National Park is the closest. Its easternmost boundary is the Indian Ocean, where wildlife interacts with the sea. But the wildlife itself is more abundant in Mikumi, which lies a good four hours' drive to the west of Dar and provides more of the "vast open plains" feeling of the Serengeti.

Some of the other best-known parks—among more than thirty that dot the country—are Gombi Stream National Park, made famous by Dr. Jane Goodall's groundbreaking work with chimpanzees, Rubondo Island National Park in Lake Victoria, and Tarangire National Park, which rounds out the northern circuit. Selous is the country's best-known game reserve, encompassing a huge area of the southeast of the country.

What sets reserves apart from national parks is that human habitation, the grazing of livestock, and the leasing of hunting blocks are permitted. National parks, in contrast, are protected areas kept as isolated as possible from human development.

THE SAFARI CODE

When in either a national park or reserve, visitors should observe some simple safari etiquette:

- Respect the privacy of the wildlife; this is their habitat.
- Beware of the animals—they are wild and unpredictable.
- Don't crowd the animals or make sudden noises or movements.
- Don't feed the animals; it upsets their diets and leads to dependency on humans.
- Keep quiet; noise disturbs the animals and may antagonize your fellow visitors.
- Stay in your vehicle at all times, except at designated picnic or walking areas.
- Keep below the maximum speed limit (25 mph / 40 kmh).
- Never drive off-road—this severely damages the habitat.
- When viewing wildlife, keep to a minimum distance of 70 ft (20 m) and pull to the side of the road to let others pass.
- Leave no litter and never light fires or discard burning objects.
- Respect the cultural heritage of Tanzania; never take pictures of the local people or their habitat without asking their permission.
- Respect the cultural traditions of Tanzania; always dress with decorum.
- Observe the rules—leave the park by dusk; never drive at night in a national park.

BEACHES

Imagine water the color of Blue Curacao lapping on sand as white as salt and palm trees leaning in the trade winds. Add warm breeze scented with exotic spices, a hammock, a grass hut with refreshments, and a colorful African sunset and it's hard not to think you've died and gone to heaven. Yet this is just an average day for the visitor on Zanzibar.

Tanzania's beaches come in a variety of shapes and colors: some are more perfect, others less so, though they are all attractive. The depth and cleanliness of the water, the quality of diving and snorkeling, accessibility, marine life, and the security situation are what differentiate the finest from the rest.

The country's best beaches are on the Zanzibar archipelago: Unguja, Pemba, and Mafia. While this is a Muslim area and guidebooks advise visitors to dress modestly, many do not. Bikinis are commonplace and female guests at some European resorts go topless. The locals make little fuss, but some see this as erosion of the Muslim culture and do take offense. Women revealing shoulders or knees is viewed even more dimly in Stonetown, where it might elicit comments or stares.

Security on Zanzibar is fairly good, though some common sense will prevent trouble. Avoid deserted beaches because muggings can and do happen and stay off the beaches at night.

The rest of Tanzania's considerable coastline is one pleasant beach after another, though some are inaccessible and others too remote to be worth the trek. Other popular beaches are to the north and south of Dar es Salaam. With the exception of Mbudya and Bongoyo Island marine parks, the best beaches are to the south of the city. The two marine parks are just a short boat ride from town and offer small slices of spectacular Indian Ocean heaven, with displays of rainbow corals and tropical fish in astounding colors.

Slip, Slop, and Slap

The Australian advertising campaign Slip, Slop, and Slap is equally relevant on Tanzania's beaches: Slip on a shirt, Slop on some sunscreen, and Slap on a hat. If you don't, expect to get burned.

PHOTOGRAPHY

Taking pictures in Tanzania can be a bit of a tricky business. Both in rural and urban areas, some people still believe that each picture taken of them steals a part of their soul. Others see it as a source of easy income and rare indeed is the Tanzanian who is content to simply have their picture taken without some recompense.

It is very highly recommended that photographers first ask for permission from their subject(s) before taking any photo depicting a person. Initially this can be tedious, especially in markets or areas where there are lots of people. But if someone takes offense or comes after you for money—a very common occurrence—having someone who gave permission is key.

Most Tanzanians will hesitate shyly about having their photograph taken, until offered some cash. Others are media savvy and will want to know if the photo will be published. Getting their signed permission to use their pictures should be possible with a little more inducement.

After some practice, and usually some expenditure, speaking to subjects before snapping away becomes entertaining and often leads to much better photographs.

chapter seven

TRAVEL, HEALTH, & SECURITY

Traveling in Tanzania is an adventure in itself. Whether within city limits, across the country, or internationally, expect the unexpected and try to keep your sense of humor.

Although the highways are reasonably well maintained, signage is inconsistent. Unfortunately, road travel in Tanzania is a sobering experience. In 2005 alone there were 17,000 injuries and 5,000 fatalities linked to accidents on the country's highways and byways—that's about thirteen deaths and forty-five injuries every day.

Schedules on any form of public transportation are based on rough guesstimates, maintenance tends to be reactive rather than proactive, and you never know who will decide to befriend you: con men or the genuinely friendly.

Tanzania's trains still carry a little of the romance of rail travel and, although they are notoriously late, they still offer a pleasant way to see the country while covering the miles.

If you can afford it, flying is where it's at. The views from above are spectacular, if somewhat detached, but it is difficult to beat the comfort, speed, and safety of an aircraft.

ARRIVING IN TANZANIA

Tired, hot, and wanting nothing more than a bed to lie on puts most arriving visitors at a significant disadvantage from the moment they step off the plane. The customs process, while slow, is usually quite straightforward, but negotiating the solicitors and hustlers at the exit is more demanding. Find a taxi driver and negotiate a price before you set off from the airport to your destination.

It's fair to assume that the value of the cab ride is probably half the initial quoted price, though drivers servicing larger airports have erected official-looking signs to support their quotes. Taxis do not usually have meters, so negotiating a price is expected regardless of where you are or where you are going. Although very much cheaper, taking public transportation is not recommended because it is distant from the airport, slow, and inconvenient.

Visiting Tanzania from a Western country requires a slightly different mind-set: keep your possessions, especially your valuables, close to your body. This is one of the world's poorest countries. Don't flash money or jewelry around. Outside the airport, make sure your luggage is secured inside the taxi and that you do not leave anything valuable on the dashboard or on your lap: snatching through open windows is common.

ROADS AND TRAFFIC

Tanzanians drive on the left. Highway infrastructure is a victim of low budgets and neglect, characterized by confusing signals, cavernous potholes, poor drainage, and roads that are impassable for all but the most robust four-wheel-drive vehicles. Added to that are unlicensed drivers and cars, trucks, and even taxis that have

never undergone a safety inspection. The end result is that most vehicles are driven by intuition, rather than according to a formal set of traffic rules—for instance, when one lane of the highway becomes jammed with traffic, drivers simply pull into the oncoming lane and continue on their way.

Poorly equipped police and an absence of speed traps means that speed goes virtually unchecked on the nation's thoroughfares, though on the arterial highways police do occasionally use radar. The speed limit in Tanzania is 50 mph (80 kph) unless otherwise posted. Those who do speed be warned.

The frequency and severity of accidents have meant that buses are no longer allowed to travel the nation's highways at night and visitors are strongly encouraged to follow suit. As with the highways, city driving is also precarious, though speeds tend to be lower.

VEHICLE RENTALS
For those willing to brave the roads, renting a car or motorcycle in Tanzania is easy. An international driver's license is best, but not essential. Rental agencies and police are satisfied with licenses from most first-world countries.

Before signing anything and driving away, read the paperwork closely. Ensure that it states clearly who is responsible for the vehicle if it breaks down, if there is an accident, and if there is any preexisting damage. Establish if there is a limit on mileage and who is responsible for filling the tank. Most importantly, establish in writing the vehicle pickup and drop-off times.

Most of these points seem obvious at first sight, but some Tanzanians rent their personal vehicles "on the side," especially motor scooters and motorcycles, and, if something goes wrong, you may suddenly find yourself liable for anything that has not been agreed to in writing.

Being Prepared
When driving in rural areas, leave prepared for the worst: a breakdown, becoming stuck, getting lost. This means packing sufficient food and drink, a warm blanket perhaps, and a first aid kit.

A "QUICK" SUNDAY AFTERNOON DRIVE

After living in wild, third-world Africa for over a decade now I have learned some very important lessons. Especially when it comes to road travel. Like, don't ever, ever, ever get into your car without water, snacks, cash, phone cards, and a fully charged phone (if you are lucky enough to be in an area with mobile phone coverage), sunscreen, blankets, and your international medical evacuation card. Seriously! And no, I am not talking here about a one-day safari into the bush. It could be as simple as a five-minute drive up the road. Since becoming a mother, the list has grown to include things like basic first aid kit, wet wipes, and toddler entertainment (coloring books, crayons, etc.).

So, when we popped out for a "quick" Sunday afternoon drive on the farm, I was prepared enough to survive in the bush for a week if necessary. Which was just as well, really . . .

As we approached it, it just looked like a shallow little stream . . . until THUMP . . . we were stuck. Tires spinning, water spraying, we all got out to have a look. It didn't look good. Miles from nowhere, and it being a Sunday no tractors out on the fields or farm staff on duty. So we tried to get the car out every way possible. All to no avail.

But, even in remotest Africa you are never alone for long. Sure enough, along came a friendly chap on a bicycle—on his way back from church. He willingly offered to help. A few minutes later, another two men appeared on foot, also en route back from church. Hemmed, one of our gardeners, also stopped to help us as he wheeled a large bag of maize meal past on his bicycle. We soon had a whole team of cheerful, willing helpers. After much effort, and over an hour, it took four strong men to "heave ho!" and the car was out. Everyone was cheering, and we told them all to go to Frank's local shop / shebeen / bar and get themselves a couple of sodas each on us . . . and we gave them a little cash as a thank you, too. I felt so bad as the men were all in their smart "Sunday clothes," which were now splattered with mud.

Lynda Hayes, *Food, Fun and Farm Life in East Africa*

Drinking and Driving
The blood/alcohol limit in Tanzania is 0.08 percent, or 80 mg of alcohol per deciliter of blood. Because of the limited nighttime police presence, drinking and driving in Tanzania remains fairly common. It is best to limit travel at night as much as possible and to take a taxi rather than drive.

In Case of Accident
Traffic accidents occur frequently in Tanzania and blame, as well as punishment, is often meted out on the spot. Any argument is often conducted

with much yelling and accusation, which typically draws large crowds of people and eventually the police.

A traffic accident is automatic grounds for being taken to jail and having to navigate the lengthy court process, so many at-fault drivers either try to settle a dispute on the spot with a payout or, if possible, continue driving without stopping. If you find yourself in a collision of any severity, head directly to the nearest police station. It is far better to sort out matters there, with due process.

PLANES, TRAINS, BUSES, AND AUTOMOBILES

Riding intercity or express buses through Tanzania can be surprisingly pleasant. Passengers sit high up in the air-conditioned cabin and have commanding views of the countryside. Tickets are usually inexpensive, the buses are new and appear well maintained, and, in the event of a collision, a bus is large and strong. The downside is that bus drivers' wages are determined by the number of passengers delivered in a day, which means flooring it to as many destinations as possible. The speed can be terrifying, especially when accompanied by passing on blind corners and other life-threatening antics.

There are also smaller buses that ply the routes between towns and make frequent stops at rural villages and hamlets. These buses are typically dilapidated old jalopies that crawl along at a moderate pace but are unlikely to make it to their

destinations without breaking down. The buses, good and bad, are almost always packed to capacity and with the windows closed it can become quite stuffy. Deodorant is as unusual as motion sickness is common.

Regardless of the bus or the destination, fellow passengers are often sociable with one another and being seated beside a Westerner is often regarded as an unmissable opportunity to practice speaking English.

With all the pros and cons, a bus is still the cheapest way to get from point A to point B, though whether you travel that way depends on how highly you value safety and comfort.

DALADALAS

Of inferior status to swift intercity buses and even the sputtering intertown buses are the lowly daladalas, which transport the workforce within Tanzania's city limits. Most often Toyota Hiace passenger vans that have long passed the age of retirement, on any given day daladalas transport about half the country.

Although daladalas are often somewhat "fragrant" and passengers are jammed together, these little buses are worth riding at least once just for the experience.

The government has legislated that their prices should not exceed a certain level, regardless of how far the passenger is traveling within a city's limits. This means it is possible to go from one end of a city to the other for a few cents.

The downside is you'll be making much of that ride with upward of twenty-seven people in a vehicle designed to carry no more than twelve. Loaded to capacity, these miniature workhorses positively bulge at the seams. Their innards have usually been stripped clean and the passengers are anything but comfortable.

With a city's entire fleet essentially on its last legs at all times, breakdowns are more than common: they're almost inevitable. Still, after a few tries, there's something strangely adventurous about riding in a daladala—just hope there isn't an accident.

A more pleasant way to get around is by rail, although Tanzania's limited rail infrastructure means it is not an option for most journeys. However, if your destination is at the other end of a track, hop aboard. Even first-class travel is reasonably inexpensive and, while the state of the cabins deteriorates on lengthy trips, it's nice to be able to walk around and exercise your legs, not to mention stretching out to sleep.

Trains also have a tendency to roll through unspoiled wilderness forests, mountains, and wide-open plains, which makes the scenery a distinctive advantage of this mode of travel. It's far more satisfying to concentrate on spotting wildlife from the train window rather than having to concentrate on the road.

The fastest and safest way to travel in Tanzania is by airplane. It's also the most expensive. But if you are with young children, or you value safety, or both, it's best to fly.

WHERE TO STAY

There are several tiers of hotels in Tanzania, from all-inclusive, five star resorts to beachside tents. In between are luxury safari lodges, mid-range hotels, small, locally owned guesthouses, and budget and backpacking accommodation. There's something to suit virtually everyone's budget and itinerary.

While the luxury resorts aim to indulge their guests' every whim, there is something predictable about them. The world over they are all from the same mold. Mid-range hotels provide a bit more variety, but for a truly unique experience every time try staying in one of Tanzania's budget guesthouses or a luxury safari lodge.

Small, informal, family-owned guesthouses are usually very inexpensive and consequently attract a mixture of customers. Owners typically live in-house and run the show. Often one or both will cook and the children or other relatives will do the cleaning. Some budget accommodation is terrific; some is positively grungy. Take a look at the rooms before putting down any money.

At the other end of the scale are luxury safari lodges. Some of these rank among Tanzania's finest experiences. Whether the accommodation is in a large tree house or in a permanent tent, raised so the balcony affords majestic views of

the African landscape, it will be a memorable stay. Despite being deep in the Tanzanian bush, lodges often offer world-class cuisine. Some have swimming pools and others have wildlife blinds so that visitors can watch the fascinating spectacle of some of nature's biggest and most ferocious creatures up close. Few moments can rate as highly as returning from a day watching animals and then relaxing on luxurious couches with a view of the terrain and ice-cold refreshment.

Permanent Accommodation

For those intending to stay longer, finding accommodation in Tanzania can be difficult, especially for visitors. Some urban and rural areas are not considered safe, which can limit options.

Leases for apartments are for a minimum of one year. At least six months' rent must be paid in advance, though landlords prefer the full year. Unless a property management firm does the work for you, it is best not to rent from overseas, sight unseen. Once in Tanzania, though, finding a place to live is only marginally easier. Substantial commissions are paid to anyone who connects tenants with landlords, so the motivation to become an "agent" is high. It is not uncommon for six or seven agents to be present at the showing of a property.

GENERAL HEALTH

The quality of health care in Tanzania is a direct reflection of how much the patient is willing to pay. The best doctors, and sometimes the only doctors, are from foreign countries. Tanzanian doctors are also highly capable, however, though they are more likely to hold clinics wherever there is a convenient spot. That might mean a dusty basement used to store old furniture!

Visiting a foreign doctor in Tanzania is relatively inexpensive, though bills add up quickly for more important procedures and if lengthy hospital stays are involved. Consulting a Tanzanian doctor is often delightfully easy on the budget.

Extra medical insurance for the traveler to Tanzania is highly recommended. In the event of a medical emergency, many insurance companies will not cover the cost of an airlift unless it is specified in the policy.

Vaccinations

It seems there is a fairly even balance between people who undergo a regimen of vaccinations before leaving home and those who skip vaccinations altogether. Most Western doctors convincingly extol the virtues of immunization.

Tanzania requires a certificate of immunization against yellow fever if the visitor has come from a country with high yellow fever risk. It is not needed if you have traveled nonstop from Europe or South Africa. A number of other immunizations against very serious diseases are also recommended, depending on the situations you anticipate experiencing in Tanzania. You would be wise to obtain medical advice well in advance of leaving home.

Other Health Warnings

Malaria is still one of Africa's—and Tanzania's—biggest killers. That's because the majority of Tanzanians can't get to a doctor easily and they can't afford expensive antimalarial pills. Only relatively recently have aid organizations and the Tanzanian government subsidized mosquito nets for locals, which has improved the malarial death rate.

In contrast, most visitors can afford all these things: doctors, medication, and nets. As a result, cases of tourists contracting malaria are much less frequent. Those who do, go straight to see a doctor and are treated, hopefully, early enough to prevent the disease from gaining a firm foothold.

Malaria is described, by those who have had it, as feeling like a particularly virulent strain of flu, magnified fivefold, plus a cold and the worst hangover you have ever had. Yet there seem to be a growing number of people who choose not to take antimalarial medication. Their choice is understandable. The older medications, such as doxycycline and mefloquine (Lariam), are rumored to have too many side effects, with questionable effectiveness, to be worthwhile. The newest antimalarial drug, Malarone, is apparently very effective with few side effects, but costs about US $5 per day.

Whichever route you choose to take, be aware that African mosquitoes are tiny, cunning, and have refined the process of stealing blood. Regardless, it is possible to have a trouble-free vacation while avoiding antimalarial medication, but nets and powerful insect repellent are highly recommended.

The tsetse fly is a tenacious beast known best for spreading sleeping sickness. The disease is caused by the entrance of parasites into the bloodstream, causing a number of unpleasant effects. Left untreated, the parasite will enter the brain and disrupt sleep patterns—hence its name—and will eventually kill the host (i.e. you).

Tsetse flies occur in inland Tanzania. The best protection against them is a good covering of light-colored clothing sprayed with a strong mixture of DEET insect repellent.

Hygiene

Hygiene in Tanzania might not be what some visitors are used to. Municipal water is not recommended for drinking or brushing teeth. Personal grooming and cleanliness are valued, but the cleaning and scrubbing of inanimate objects, such as walls, kitchens, vehicles, and so forth, is generally more relaxed, either because of ignorance or due to economic shortfalls.

City streets often flood during the rainy seasons because of accumulated refuse and the sporadic electricity supply means that even businesses equipped with refrigeration cannot necessarily keep chilled goods at appropriate temperatures. Luckily, most shops have backup generators. If possible, avoid the ones that don't.

VISITORS AND THE LAW

The judicial system is a combination of British common law, East African customary law, and Islamic law. Tanzanians are often disparaging of their legal system. Some quip that lawsuits never succeed because the people launching them die before their cases are ever resolved.

Nonetheless, running afoul of the law in Tanzania is nothing to be sneezed at. A car accident, for instance, is automatic grounds for jail. In this situation, bond or bail can be granted at the police's or magistrate's discretion and all cases must be brought before a court.

Being a policeman in Tanzania is viewed as an honorable position, though it is poorly paid. This lays the police open to bribery and corruption as much as anyone else. The government says it is committed to stamping out the corruption economy and the consequences of conviction are severe, so bribes are rarely, if ever, openly discussed or demanded outright. But there's no mistaking the meaning of, say, "You can make this easy for both of us." These suggestions are most often delivered in the event of a driving infraction or other misdemeanor.

One archaic law that catches many visitors off guard is a remnant of the socialist days of Nyerere: it stipulates that no photographs may be taken of bridges, airports, railways, or government and military installations. Though this law has been greatly relaxed in recent years, it is still occasionally enforced by security officials and can lead to a fine or the confiscation of photography equipment.

For those unwilling—or unable—to pay an on-the-spot fine, it's best to determine the amount of the penalty and then suggest going to the police station to settle the matter. At this point most police will choose to deliver an admonishment before moving on to easier targets.

In addition to police, Tanzania has a great many security guards. Almost every home and every business is patrolled by one or more, often armed, security personnel. Though most carry a gun and dress like commandos, they have limited powers. In the case of a disagreement, keep a cell phone handy and the telephone number of the local police programmed into it.

chapter eight

BUSINESS BRIEFING

BUSINESS CULTURE

While Tanzanians are not typically ambitious in the business sense, there are some notable exceptions. Those with natural business acumen and particularly those who could afford a decent education do well in Tanzania. But it's not easy. Russian and Chinese businesspeople are competing increasingly for a share of the economy— primarily in telecommunications, construction, and mining—against South Africans, Arabs, South Asians, and Europeans. These are the people that visitors to Tanzania will most likely deal with at high corporate levels.

At the street level, there are countless small-scale businessmen and shopkeepers who keep the country bustling along. Taxi drivers, tradesmen, restaurateurs, and dealers of all shapes and sizes are still the face of indigenous Tanzanian commerce.

Tanzanians are also the backbone of the national workforce. Government is almost exclusively run by native Tanzanians, while more and more aspiring businessmen are studying overseas and returning home with foreign educations and foreign commercial ideals, which they are translating into business ventures of all kinds.

Though times are gradually changing, women traditionally play, at best, supporting roles in business. As a result, visiting businesswomen may occasionally find themselves having to deal with stereotyping or discrimination.

Business Hours

Bank opening hours are 8:30 a.m.–3:00 p.m., Monday to Friday. Government office hours are 8:00 a.m.–4:00 p.m., Monday to Friday. Shops are open 8:30 a.m.–5:30 p.m. or 6:00 p.m., Monday to Friday, and 8:30 a.m.–1:00 p.m. on Saturdays.

In addition to regular banking hours, most foreign exchange bureaus remain open until 5:00 p.m., Monday to Friday and until noon on Saturday. Many shops and offices close for one to two hours between noon and 2:00 p.m. and, especially in the Muslim coastal areas, on Friday afternoons for attendance at mosque services.

Contacts and Networking

In Tanzania it is important to establish a personal relationship before getting down to business because Tanzanians see the business itself as secondary. In such a relationship, the emphasis is on character and behavior; business begins only when dealing with someone whom they regard as a friend they can trust and respect.

There are a number of ways to make business contacts in Tanzania. First, read the local newspaper. The larger cities have English-language newspapers that run ads for clubs and organizations aimed at people with common interests. Clubs might be based on nationality, hobby, or sport. Soccer (football) in particular is a game that transcends racial and economic barriers. While joining the rugby club might not seem an obvious choice, postgame beers in the team's favorite bar provide a great opportunity to network. Some international organizations also have branches in Tanzania, including the famous Hash House Harriers running club and the Rotary Club.

The Internet in Tanzania is relatively new and Web sites are beyond the budgets of most, but it is worth checking to see if there are clubs of interest in the area.

Churches and mosques are also good places to network. While talking business during services is not approved of, following services, on the church or mosque steps, is a good time to meet people.

Adjust to "Swahili Time"

Tanzanians' interpretation of punctuality is very liberal (see also Chapter Two). If a meeting is scheduled for 9:00 a.m., and you arrive on time, it's almost guaranteed you'll be the only person to do so. Arriving within a half hour of the scheduled meeting time is considered punctual and being an hour or more late is acceptable.

If a meeting involves a board or a number of people, expect them to arrive sporadically.

The Tanzanian interpretation of time is perhaps one of the most difficult cultural differences for visitors to adjust to. It can be enormously frustrating for arriving businesspeople with much to do and little time, but insisting on punctuality will do more to alienate Tanzanians than to change age-old habits.

Arranging a Meeting

Though calling ahead to announce an intended visit is standard, it is usually more effective simply to arrive at an office in person. Doing so will, to some degree, eliminate the problem of punctuality, though visitors run the risk of finding that their contact is out.

In offices where there are no secretaries, it is considered perfectly fine just to walk in on the person you're intending to meet. It is also common for several people to enter and leave the office while you are conducting your meeting.

Tanzanians place far more stock in face time than in electronic communication; the recent arrival of cell phones brought with it the country's first reliable telecommunications network, although minutes are very expensive. And while most people have an e-mail account, few have dedicated access to the Internet. E-mails may go unanswered for days or weeks, if there is a reply at all.

Presentations

Presentations should combine slick technology with short, punchy points. Humor and entertainment will always win the day over drab content loaded with statistics. When presenting to a group, speak to them as a whole, but at key points make eye contact with the most significant players. Be brief. Attention spans tend to be short and contract rapidly in the heat of the afternoon.

It is important for foreigners to remember that phone calls take precedence over all other business. If a phone rings during a presentation, it is considered absolutely acceptable to answer it and conduct a conversation for several minutes. Often this is a noisy distraction and can be disconcerting for those who are not used to it. This is an ordinary occurrence, however, and no cause to take offense.

Tanzanians will typically wait until the end of a presentation to begin asking questions. It is not a bad idea to hand out a printed conclusion consisting of several complex points.

BUSINESS ETIQUETTE

As a form of respect when introducing themselves, and in discussion, Tanzanians will often refer to each other by their first names preceded by "Mr."—for example "Mr. George" to address a man named George Lilanga. As we've seen, handshakes can be drawn out affairs and getting a

Tanzanian to open up is most easily done by complimenting the country or the government.

Dress Code

Tanzanians take pride in their appearance. Though they might not have much money, they will show up for business in clean, pressed shirts and long pants or skirts. When not clean shaven, men will wear neatly trimmed facial hair. Women typically sport a fashionably conservative hairdo and sensible shoes.

Even those from the lower classes make every effort to wear clean clothing. It is important for them to look well-groomed. As for shoes, Tanzanians frown upon the use of flip-flops outside of the house as they are normally used only in the bathroom.

On the coast, men often wear a short-sleeved jacket and shirt with matching pants. In general, men do not wear shorts (normally only primary school-aged boys) and women wear clothing that covers both their knees and their shoulders. Most men carry a handkerchief for mopping their brows on the hottest days.

In the cooler areas, around the north (Moshi, Arusha) and in the south, a jacket may be expected. Rural area or not, work clothes are still expected to look sharp, though the standard will be more relaxed. Though Tanzanian women do not normally wear slacks, this is becoming more common with the younger generation.

WOMEN IN BUSINESS

It is rare to find women in the upper echelons of business in Tanzania. At work, women will often have lower status than men and are more likely to be asked to make coffee and take care of tasks that are not in their job description. They are also more likely to feel intimidated by their supervisors and sometimes their colleagues.

The good news is that it is becoming gradually more common for women to hold traditionally respected professional positions, though either lower in the hierarchy or in other fields. Many of these women fight a daily battle against sexism. As a man conducting business with such women, it is best to avoid all physical contact after the initial handshake. Be careful also that compliments are not misconstrued.

Businesswomen visiting Tanzania are usually treated with more respect than their Tanzanian counterparts, though sexism is almost inevitable to some degree in a male-dominated society. Immodest behavior by a woman, such as excessive drinking or revealing attire, will mean she forfeits all respect.

CORRUPTION—A "SOCIAL VICE"

Tanzanians don't like to say no. In many offices, businesses, or government services, this will be translated into "tomorrow" (*kesho*). This can be a delaying tactic—or a subtle way of asking for something extra: a bribe.

President Kikwete has sworn to stamp out corruption. His public denunciation of this "social vice" is driven in part by pressure from donor countries, but there are other factors that are perhaps even more pressing. As Kikwete said when announcing his government's war against graft: "Since corruption is a social vice *wananchi* [citizens] abhor, it can push the people to turn against their government, especially when they realize it violated their individual rights and liberties. With excessive corruption people lose confidence in their government, leading to conflicts that can impact negatively on security, national cohesion, and social stability."

Kikwete has overseen the dismissal and resignation of some of the country's top political leaders, including the governor of Tanzania's central bank and even the prime minister. The fact these events continue to happen is an indication of how ingrained corruption is, from the lowest public official, right to the very top.

It is difficult to measure the impact of such high profile dismissals. Over morning coffee some Tanzanians express surprise that such a high-ranking official could fall from grace, yet they are so used to it that there is a large measure of acceptance, maybe shading in to apathy about it. Consequently there is no immediate difference in the way things are run. Some officials processing visa extension applications still obliquely suggest ways of speeding up the process, while traffic police continue to levy cash-only fines on the spot. Daily newspapers run stories of corruption on a huge scale.

Whether promises to stamp out corruption are just for appearances or if it really is on the way out is a matter of some debate. In the meantime, there are a number of ways to respond to suggestions such as "You can help me help you." Tanzanians handle such situations with a smile and a sense of humor. They discuss the possible amount of the bribe, weigh its cost against the promised benefit, negotiate some more, explain their position, and eventually choose to pay or not. Once negotiations have begun, however, there is always the risk that not paying will lead to even slower service.

The best way to deflect or decline such a demand is to refuse to understand the reference. Feign ignorance. Say that you don't understand. This is fairly easy because Tanzanians never come right out and say "pay a bribe." It is always cloaked in relatively obscure language (see also under *Kitu Kidogo* in Chapter 2).

It is important to remember that the reactions of Tanzanians can vary greatly: some are willing to go to extremes to help complete strangers while others expect a return for even the simplest tasks.

NEGOTIATIONS

There are no set rules for negotiations in Tanzania other than that they should always be conducted in a friendly, spirited manner.

Tanzanian organizations often have a clearly defined structure that usually involves the highest-ranking officer as the central decision maker, often the founder of the organization, who consequently drives and directs it. During complex or lengthy negotiations, this person will

most often attend the process. If they do not, expect the final decision to take time coming.

Once the negotiations begin, if things become exasperating or seem like a waste of time, simply excuse yourself politely and leave. At this point, the true test of a bargaining situation is whether the other person at the table calls you back. Very few will pass up the chance of making a sale or closing a deal, no matter how thin the profit. On the other hand, if the other party does not call you back, chances are your demands are unrealistic. Of course, there's always the possibility that too many other high rollers have come through and the stakes have changed.

CONTRACTS AND FULFILLMENT

Contracts between Tanzanians are frequently verbal, though this is determined in part by the level of trust between the parties and the amount of money at stake. An agreement will be made in front of the people they respect most, such as wife, relatives, and friends. The commitment or promise made tends to be respected more because everyone present is regarded as a witness to the occasion.

> **LOST REVENUE – THE COST OF PAPERLESS CONTRACTS**
> The Tanzanian government found that millions of dollars' worth of timber revenue was being lost each year in verbal agreements [between landowners, logging contractors and exporters], a result of poor governance and rampant corruption, resulting in illegal logging and exports of forest products. The annual loss of timber revenue in Tanzania is equivalent to the cost of building more than 10,000 secondary school classrooms or providing a quarter of Tanzanians with mosquito nets, said TRAFFIC's Simon Milledge, lead author of the report.
>
> Media release, *Tanzania Government Tackles Forestry Corruption*, TRAFFIC International

Foreigners engaging in business might well be advised to hire a local lawyer to help negotiate the minutiae of Tanzania's statutory laws and contract obligations. Although written contracts are regarded more as a Western formality, and therefore tolerated rather than observed, they do reduce the possibility of misunderstanding and carry more weight should disputes ever reach the court stage. In large-scale business dealings where greater amounts of finance are involved, it is more likely that contracts will be a hybrid of written and verbal. A written contract will be drawn up and signed initially but, as circumstances change, further agreements are likely to be verbal.

Should disputes arise over a written or verbal agreement, the best solution—because it's fastest and cheapest—is to settle the matter through dialogue and ongoing renegotiations. The running joke (as cited previously) says both parties would have expired long before the courts decided anything, so it's all the more important in any business disagreement to keep the relationship of trust going.

DEALING WITH GOVERNMENT
Government in Tanzania, as in most of the developing world, is an unwieldy and inefficient bureaucracy, yet it exerts a lot of control over the business environment. It appoints boards of directors to public companies, or companies that are partly state owned. Sometimes it will bypass the bidding process and instead appoint a particular company to take the job. The CEOs of privately run companies work closely with federal ministers.

When negotiating with the government, it's worth keeping in mind that things can be vetoed from the top. Information in government institutions is tightly controlled so anticipate unexpected decisions when negotiating a contract.

What's more, the often hidden hand of the government may combine with the nature of Tanzanian society—its extended families and the priority they enjoy— so it can be that jobs, contracts, or general preference is extended on a who-you-are or a who-you-know basis, rather than purely on competence or value.

GETTING DOWN TO BUSINESS
Tanzanians conduct business at a slower pace than you may be used to. Computers are still relatively rare, so few people use e-mail. Until the arrival of cell

phones, entire cities—even Dar es Salaam—had just a handful of telephone lines. Even with cell phones, pay-as-you-go credit may infuriatingly run out mid-conversation and phones are frequently lost or stolen. Add to that the Tanzanian preference to say "sure" or "no problem" and so overextend themselves, and the result is that even the most industrious Tanzanians do not follow schedules closely.

Because of the widespread poverty, what may seem like small amounts of money to a Westerner can have much greater value for a Tanzanian. Consequently, even the smallest transactions involve time-consuming negotiations as prices are rarely fixed.

This leads to a totally different business culture. Visitors who arrive hoping to attend several meetings, host a conference, and finalize a report in a single day will probably end up frustrated. It is not the way business is done in Tanzania. Your best course is to let go of expectations and let the day simply unfold. It is this relative lack of control over the events and productivity of a day that causes culture shock in many visitors.

The qualities most highly valued in managers and supervisors in Tanzania are education, experience, people skills, and work ethic. The most successful managers are those who are open to new ideas and show their leadership skills when it really matters. Most Tanzanians hold in high regard those superiors who can make difficult decisions and stand by them.

Tanzanians will often seek feedback on their performance. However, for more direct information and guidance they will often turn to their colleagues, for fear that checking repeatedly with a supervisor may make them look unqualified or incompetent. If a Tanzanian employee believes that a proposal runs the risk of not being accepted, they will often try first to get support from colleagues.

STAFF AND THE WORKPLACE

Tanzanians judge a person by their personality, ability to get along with others, flexibility, and capacity to see tasks through to their conclusion. Status is also very important, so if a manager or other senior figure invites you home for dinner or another social event it is polite to accept and attend, even if only briefly.

Work-related problems are best resolved privately as any public confrontation would be regarded as humiliating. In Tanzania there may be very few clues that a colleague is upset with you. Many people hide their feelings, especially in the presence of foreigners and supervisors. But they may stop talking, or avoid your presence, or make themselves busy; normal conversations may turn into arguments or hot debate more frequently. It is as important to listen to what is *not* being said as to what is.

Foreigners are almost as likely as Tanzanians to be approached to hire a family member at work (or at home). Shrewd business people in Tanzania never hire exclusively from the same tribe or area, even if those applicants are highly competent.

An employer is not obliged to keep an employee, though firing someone is a delicate matter. They may delay things, rather than inflict a flat-out rejection. Low-paid employees may be told that there is no work for a few days and that they will be called when there is more, rather than being explicitly fired.

chapter nine

COMMUNICATING

LANGUAGE

The official language is Swahili (Kiswahili in the language itself). English is the main language of commerce, administration, and higher education. Arabic is widely spoken in Zanzibar, and there are several dozen local languages.

Most Tanzanians are bilingual, speaking both their local language and Swahili, if not trilingual, with English as a third. As most people use their national language in daily life rather than English, they may be a little awkward at first when switching to English for you.

Swahili is ever-evolving and dynamic. Colloquial expressions can appear in use one day and others vanish the next. Most of these are single words used in abstract ways or short, humorous sentences. A contemporary example is *shwari*, meaning that things are fine going into the future. This is a relatively recent response to the greeting *habari* ("What news?"). Another fun example is *poa chizi kama ndizi* ("I'm as fresh as a banana") in response to the common and informal *poa* (meaning "What's up?").

English is widely understood in urban areas and to a lesser degree in the countryside. Tanzanians tend to speak Oxford English rather than American ghetto slang, and most of those who speak English do so quite well and are easily understandable. General conversation in English is liberally strewn with Swahili words and phrases.

The fastest way into Tanzanian culture is to overcome the language barrier, which means learning Swahili. Doing so will tremendously increase the number of people you interact with and will help you get to know them.

BODY LANGUAGE

The Tanzanians are a tactile and expressive people. Face, body language, and tone of voice are important in conversation, and laughter, physical contact, or expressions of interest are sure signs the listener is engaged. They can be quite animated when listening to a story, and will make reassuring sounds to the speaker, such as a quick exhalation of breath to mean "Yes, I hear you."

Standing at a distance from a speaker, we have seen, is a sign that they are not welcome. (This does not apply to someone who is simply rushed, and takes a few moments regardless for a quick exchange before warmly suggesting a lengthier meeting at a later time.)

Eye contact carries great importance, especially during official conversations and any transaction involving trust. Avoiding eye contact implies you are not telling the whole truth or are not committed to the discussion. In contrast, prolonged eye contact with a person of the opposite sex, especially with a female friend or stranger, is unwelcome and regarded as an invasion of privacy or downright rude. Most Tanzanian women find being stared at embarrassing, as it can have sexual overtones. In a society that frowns on public displays of affection a blatantly lingering gaze reflects poor manners. While eye contact is expected between people of seniority and Westerners, Tanzanians are expected to avert their gaze from superiors.

If someone cracks a joke while chatting and others laugh, then it's normal for the listeners— even if they're complete strangers—to stretch out a hand so the speaker can clap it. This "high five" gesture is a way of acknowledging a clever turn of phrase or the quality of the tale and may take place more than once in a longish story. If for some reason their or your right hand is unavailable, put forward a wrist, lower arm, shoulder, or upper arm. Touching hands during conversation among friends, or even office colleagues, is common.

A remnant of colonial days, pointing with your finger at any one is considered very rude, as is summoning with a crooked finger or beckoning with the palm up (you should always beckon with the palm down). Emitting a loud hiss to attract someone's attention is considered extremely impolite, though some Tanzanians do it nevertheless. (It is the sound typically made to call to a prostitute.)

Khanga *Diplomacy*

Conflict, especially in the workplace, is generally dealt with subtly, rather than conducted in the open. Women sometimes wear *khangas* (two identical rectangular pieces of cloth that have a colorful design, a border, and a saying in Swahili written on one of the long sides) to deliver a message. A good example of this would be wearing a *khanga* that says "If gossip was money, some would be rich" while passing by a gossiping neighbor. *Khangas* are often given as gifts and chosen specifically for their message to fit the occasion, such as "Wishing you all the best" for someone who is departing.

HUMOR

Tanzanians like making fun of themselves and others. They delight in jokes based on puns, double entendres, or ambiguous turns of phrase, such as one about the European plantation owner who tells his Tanzanian employee to make coffee. The word coffee sounds like the Swahili *kofe*, which means "slap." The employee approaches and gives his shocked employer an almighty slap.

Tanzanians enjoy other people's mistakes, especially those made when learning Swahili. Something as simple as confusing the word "fine" with "banana" can cause gales of laughter.

Jokes offend few people as long as they do not refer to one's immediate family, especially one's mother, sister, or wife. Gentle chiding is acceptable and if done cleverly can provoke great merriment.

Some jokes point to the cultural differences with neighboring countries. Like . . . A Tanzanian man is visiting Nairobi. He goes into a bar and orders a beer, saying: *Naomba Tusker* (which translates roughly as "I would like a Tusker," or "a Tusker please"). The bartender looks at him and replies, "We don't give to beggars here." The point lies in the difference between Tanzanian and Kenyan Swahili: Tanzanian Swahili is much more polite, and Tanzanians in general are regarded as being more courteous. Kenyans would order a beer saying: *Nipe Tusker* ("Give me Tusker"). In Kenya, the polite *naomba* might be used by a beggar to ask for money.

TOPICS OF CONVERSATION

Tanzanians feel that it is important to lay the groundwork for a conversation before launching directly into whatever is to be talked about. While in some cultures this might seem like an unnecessary preamble, it is not polite to interrupt it even if they've been speaking for some time.

Good topics of conversation are sports or current events, especially the latest stories featured in magazines or tabloid papers. These are often about witch doctors or supernatural events, or sometimes war in other countries.

While Tanzanians don't flaunt their political views, perhaps a hangover from Nyerere's one-party-state days, discussing politics is common among people who know each other well. But even those who shy away from talking politics are usually willing to discuss government policies,

At Heaven's Gate

A Saudi, a Goan, and a Tanzanian were in a terrible car accident. They were all taken to the same emergency room, but all three of them died before they arrived. Just as they were about to put the toe tag on the Saudi, he stirred and opened his eyes. Astonished, the doctors and nurses asked him what happened.

"Well, I remember the crash, and then there was a beautiful light," said the Saudi. "Then the Tanzanian and the Goan and I were standing at the gates of heaven. St. Peter approached us and said that we were all too young to die and that for a donation of 1,000/- we could return to earth. So, of course, I pulled out my wallet and gave him the 1,000/- and the next thing I knew I was back here."

"That's amazing!" exclaimed one of the doctors. "But what happened to the other two?" "Last I saw of them," replied the Saudi, "the Goan was haggling over the price, and the Tanzanian was waiting for someone to pay for him."

taxes, public scandals, and even embezzlement, so long as they are already in the media.

In general, Tanzanians do not like discussing money matters. Nor is it polite to question someone about what they do for a living, especially at a first meeting. Instead, Tanzanians will try to establish how to relate to you by asking what part of the country you live in and what your religion is. Visitors will also be asked how long they've been in the country, where they're from, and what they think of Tanzania—whatever length of time they may have been there. As we've seen, Tanzanians are proud of their country and don't like negative remarks about it.

PROPER ACKNOWLEDGMENT

Depending on the workplace, people address each other by their surnames or married names, and in less formal environments by their first names. For those who are well acquainted or familiar, or of the same age group, the first name is usually used, especially among women.

At home, between friends, and in informal contexts, Tanzanians address each other with familial titles that correspond to their age: adult women will be *mama* (mother), older women *bibi* (grandmother), younger women *dada* (sister), adult men *baba* (father), elderly men *babu* (grandfather), or *mzee* (dignified man). People may also call restaurant servers *rafiki* (friend).

When addressing someone by name it is best to use their surname and let them state what they would like to be called.

THE MEDIA

The main source of information in Tanzania is the press. Considering the relatively high rate of illiteracy, Tanzanians are avid newspaper readers. In big cities such as Dar es Salaam there are dozens of newspapers in both Swahili and English. In rural areas there are fewer, but there is always at least one newspaper to be had.

Tanzania's constitution guarantees every citizen the right to freedom of opinion and expression. However, the Newspaper Act of 1976 also allows authorities within the government—including the president—the power to prohibit publications that are deemed not to be in the nation's best interests. Freedom House, a US organization that bills itself as a voice for democracy and freedom around the world, has declared that the media in Tanzania is only partly free. Despite the constitution's guarantee of free speech, there are examples of the government repressing information. Self-censorship is often practiced as a result of the state's intimidation of reporters.

Self-censorship is most apparent in questioning election outcomes. This is a sensitive topic for the government, which goes to great lengths to appear to be within legal boundaries when interfering with the freedom of the press. In 2001 the government shut down *The Tanzanian*, one of the more aggressive Swahili papers, on the grounds that the publisher was not a Tanzanian national. Such things happen with sufficient frequency to remind those in print to be wary and sensitive.

Still, Tanzanian newspapers can be quite critical in their reporting, though any negative comment on individuals in government is very measured. Inefficiency is a safer target than misconduct, as are bureaucratic inadequacy and poor social conditions.

Despite its reluctance to launch any real attack on government, Tanzania's press revels in lurid stories of sex scandals, murders, and crimes involving obscene acts, often sparing no detail.

Corruption in journalism is sometimes discussed in the media (which takes considerable pride in being above this sort of thing), and stories do circulate of journalists either omitting coverage or manipulating facts in exchange for a fat manila envelope. How much money actually changes hands and how frequently this occurs is difficult to pinpoint.

The appeal of newspapers over television to Tanzanians lies in their affordability and the fact they don't rely on an often sporadic municipal power supply or erratic signal reception. Television is popular, however, with those who can afford it, and radios even more so. The numbers are interesting: there are three television stations and an estimate of just 103,000 television sets. That is 2.8 televisions per 1,000 Tanzanians. In contrast, there are twenty-five radio stations and an estimated 8,800,000 radio receivers—a total of 242.9 per 1,000.

TELEPHONES

Landlines

While not entirely accurate, the joke that the number of dedicated phone lines in Tanzania can be counted on the fingers of one hand has a ring of truth to it. The communications infrastructure has not been widely developed, presumably because of a lack of funding. The Tanzania Telecommunications Company Ltd (TTCL), the state-owned service provider, operates all pay phones and landlines. While expensive landlines have basically been relegated to the bottom of the priority list, they are still useful for pay phones, where residents and visitors can make local and long-distance calls without having to buy a cell phone. The disadvantage is that they tend to be located in a dwindling number of shops offering this service, a few hotels, and outside post offices and some government agencies. For anyone staying for longer than two weeks, it's worth investing in an inexpensive, disposable cell phone.

Cell Phones and Text Messaging

Though cell phone service is reliable, it is also very expensive. Monthly plans are all but unheard of, with the majority of the population purchasing minutes in a pay-as-you-go format. Unfortunately, the minutes frequently run out and connections are then abruptly severed in mid-conversation.

Cell phones in Tanzania are unlocked. One benefit is that a phone purchased in Tanzania can be used in almost any country, simply by installing a new SIM card. The drawback is that thieves can take a phone, insert a new card, and resell it in less time than it takes the victim to realize they've been robbed. As a result, cell phone theft is a hot ticket in Tanzania.

Charges from cell phones are high. It is almost as expensive to call your next-door neighbor as to call from Tanzania to somewhere in North America or Europe. Text messaging is the preferred method of reducing the cost of calls, though Tanzanians have taken this one step further. The latest trend is to call the person they wish to speak to and hang up just as they answer.

The theory is that the recipient sees they have missed a call and then calls the number back once curiosity kicks in. It seems to work.

While they are expensive and coverage is sometimes questionable, cell phones are widely regarded as doing more to usher Africa into the twenty-first century than any other single thing. Business happens faster and is more reliable and fair through the ability of buyers and sellers to communicate directly with each other.

While cell phones are paving the way for modern business methods, they're also facilitating other types of enterprise. Young people, who were once unable to fraternize because of cultural traditions or distance, can now do so almost effortlessly.

THE INTERNET

The Internet is a wildly growing phenomenon in Tanzania, driven largely by the young. Most schools have at least one computer, so children are growing up familiar with the concept, if not necessarily proficient in its use. However, there is a technological divide within Tanzania.

The most frequent users of Internet cafés are students and young people. Women make up 40 percent of Internet café users in urban areas, but just 25 percent in rural areas (pointing in this instance to a "gender digital divide").

Most young professionals have an e-mail address, though Web sites for businesses are still relatively rare. Some businesses have Web sites that are perpetually under construction and reveal little or nothing of the operation.

Most towns have at least one Internet café, though connections tend to be slow and unreliable. As a testament to the growing popularity of the Net, many of the computer keyboards in Internet cafés have smooth blank keys where the letters have worn off. Many of the luxury hotels offer data ports in the rooms and Wi-Fi hot spots. It is here that a visitor is most likely to find real high-speed connections.

MAIL

Mailing letters in Tanzania is easy and efficient. It's also inexpensive. But the demand for "snail mail" is waning in the face of burgeoning Internet use and its attendant e-mail culture, faxes, and cell phones.

Shipping parcels in Tanzania is another matter. It is brutally slow, inefficient, and unsafe, and few people bother with the hassle. Even those who receive parcels of personal effects from overseas are sometimes asked to pay "duty" before they are released. Few courier companies operate in Tanzania because, without addresses, door-to-door deliveries are difficult. Some couriers operate from a central depot, where clients can send and receive parcels.

CONCLUSION

Tanzania and its cities are what a visitor makes of them. There's culture, fashion, and style, and people who are swept up in the new, money-driven ethos, but there is also a mass of people who are struggling against abject poverty. The contrast can leave you trying to reconcile head with heart, logic with feeling, fact with myth. With their wealth of history and culture, how can Tanzanians be so poor? Despite their poverty, how can they have the brightest smiles of all?

Outside Tanzania's urban boundaries is another country entirely—a broad mixture of landscapes, animals, and people. The Hadzabe live a life unchanged since the dawn of humankind;

the tall, slim Maasai are an exclamation of color; lions rule the savanna; and poisonous spiders find refuge in the cool mountains. Rising above them all is Mount Kilimanjaro, a Tanzanian icon. To stand on its summit in the early morning is an experience that will take your breath away. Down on the coastal plain few things can match the equatorial warmth in the evening, or the heady scent of frangipani on the wind.

The goal of this book, however, has been to help you to understand and appreciate this beautiful country's greatest natural resource: the Tanzanians. Although we have explored their daily efforts to improve themselves, and the competing demands of tradition and modernity on Tanzanian society, we have also seen what makes them so peaceful, stable, and warm. The life-affirming values of *undugu* are the unique, defining quality of this magnificent people.

Further Reading

Caplan, Patricia. *African Voices, African Lives: Personal Narratives from a Swahili Village.* London and New York: Routledge, 1997.

Goscinny, Yves. *Tribute to George Lilanga.* Dar es Salaam: Tanzanian East African Development and Communication Foundation, 2001.

Hayes, Lynda. *Food, Fun and Farm Life in East Africa.* http://foodfunfarm.blogspot.com

Indakwa, John and Ballali, Daudi. *Beginner's Swahili.* New York: Hippocrene Books, 1995.

McCulla, Patricia. *Tanzania (Major World Nations).* New York: Chelsea House Publications, 1998.

Mercer, Graham. *Bagamoyo, Town of Palms.* Dar es Salaam: Times Offset, 2007.

Pitcher, Gemma and Javed Jafferji. *Magic of Zanzibar.* Zanzibar: Gallery Publications, 2005.

Theroux, Paul. *Dark Star Safari.* London: Penguin Books, 2002.

culture smart! tanzania

Index

culture smart! tanzania

Acknowledgment

Thanks to Sarah B., whose love of adventure helped make
this book possible.